Living Letters from Heaven

Consoling
Comforting
Coaching

Rose Sieber

Living Letters from Heaven,
Consoling, Comforting, Coaching
ISBN: 978-1-941173-53-4
Copyright © 2022 by Rose Reggiacorte Sieber

Published by
Olive Press Messianic and Christian Publisher
olivepresspublisher.com

Printed in the USA

Cover design by Olive Press
Cover photos © 2021 by Hans Seiber, the author's husband

In honor to God, all pronouns referring to the Trinity are capitalized; satan's names are not.

All Scriptures are taken from *The King James Version,* (public domain) with grammar and spelling updated with these types of changes: thee and thou to you, hath to has, cometh to comes, Ghost to Spirit, etc.

Living Letters from Heaven

Consoling, Comforting, Coaching

Rose Sieber

OlivePress
צהר זית
Publisher

Dear Reader,

Hoping you enjoy reading "my mail" from the Lord Jesus. By listening to and communicating with His Holy Spirit, I've been able to be richly counseled, encouraged, and strengthened to live life to the fullest. I hope you will find the same in my letters, and be invited to receive your own personally designed "mail" as well. Life in the Spirit of God is the best, most delightfully creative life you can live. I highly recommend it.

This little book of letters to me from my Heavenly Father is a part of His restoration of my life. I lost my natural father around age three. This caused a great void in my life, as well as much trouble as I tried to fill it. When I discovered that I could know and enjoy my Heavenly Father through Jesus the Messiah, He restored the Father-daughter relationship I had lost. My hope is, that this book will help restore and enrich all sons and daughters who read it.

Lovingly, Rose

My Child,

Out of all your life experiences, I distill an elixir of hope and peace for others. This oil brings My Presence and voice to reality for many. I desire to multiply My influence into places you cannot imagine. Enjoy the prospect of how I am using your life experiences and pen to bless and grow and delight many. My Spirit is a comforting teacher who uses countless ambassadors to reach all corners of the world by every good means available on earth. Be assured I am giving you a living legacy.

Dear Child,

Do not question the writing of this book, "Living Letters." I always have much to say to My children. In your world, I need your pen to place it where others can discover Me. So, enjoy the process and collecting. Do not doubt its worth or readability. As always, the outcome and results are in My hands. I have always used words to create and lead My people. Reading never grows old nor is it empty of purpose. Write for Me with confidence.

"...Write this for a memorial in a book...." Exodus 17:14

Spring

Dear Child,

Draw into your inner heart's fire on these days of quiet repose. Silently fulfill the simple tasks of everyday life. Notice all the small blessings of My provision to delight your senses. The fragrance of a wood fire, the chirping of birds, the steam from a cup of tea. I make your life on earth so rich and full of meaning. You feel no need to strive for wealth, position and influence. I am all these and more to you. What I assign to you is more than enough for fruitful, peaceful satisfaction.

"For He satisfies the longing soul, and fills the hungry soul with goodness." Psalm 107:9

"For what is a man profited, if he shall gain the whole world, and lose his own soul? or what shall a man give in exchange for his soul?" Matthew 16:26

Dear Child,

Truly, it is My Spirit in you, and among My children as you are together, that is the deep desire of all the world. For this I created you in family and people groups, that no one need be lonely and isolated.

This is my answer to all wars, disputes, and divisions. All great differences are resolved and dissolved in that I created all people in My image for My companionship. Wherever My Gospel is preached and obeyed there is My peaceable fellowship, belief, and agreement with My Word. This is the harmony and freedom I desire for My children.

"So God created man in His own image, in the image of God created He him; male and female created He them." Genesis 1:27

"For where two or three are gathered together in My Name, there am I in the midst of them." Matthew 18:20

Dear Child,

I am the wellspring of your well being. All the good within and around you is sourced in Me. In quiet communion with Me, you experience the reality of your inner person where I dwell and order your life under My hand. Truly, this is the experience of being in My Kingdom. I make you rich in all that's real, available, and glorious. Receive, reflect, and give generously at every opportunity. Many hunger and thirst for Me and My righteousness. Be a gentle, sweet source that others can taste.

"O taste and see that the LORD is good: blessed is the man that trusts in Him." Psalm 34:8

"Blessed are they which do hunger and thirst after righteousness: for they shall be filled." Matthew 5:6

Dear Child,

Depending on Me first and completely requires My divinely inspired courage. Many other voices will attempt to tell you where to find help in need. Quietly wait and listen to My counsel and revelation. I see the complexity of many problems and the order in which they're best solved. Some of them you can do nothing about. Your steps are ordered by Me and I will not abandon you. Approach your needs from the standpoint of, "What am I to learn and adjust from this?" I am the teacher leader. Take much hope from this.

"God is our refuge and strength, a very present help in trouble." Psalm 46:1

"The steps of a good man are ordered by the LORD: and he delights in his way." Psalm 37:23

Dear Child,

I give you beauty for ashes. Reflect on the burned-out years of useless activity without Me. What remains is ashes that return to nourish the earth. Let the ashes of your memories and regrets be food for reflection as you meditate on the truth of My Word. Much can be gained from your experience and learning in this way. It is My economy to use all things for good in some way for those who love Me. Out of this will spring My joy unspeakable. A wise Father desires maturity with beautiful joy for His children.

"To appoint unto them that mourn in Zion, to give unto them beauty for ashes, the oil of joy for mourning, the garment of praise for the spirit of heaviness...." Isaiah 61:3

"And we know that all things work together for good to them that love God, to them who are the called according to His purpose." Romans 8:28

Dear Child,

Yes, you agree with Me. I am the complete and only hope for mankind's dark and lost and confused condition. I gladly and obediently gave My life for once and for always redemption. Grieve not, but look to the hope and rejoice for all those who do know, love, and follow Me. What you see in the world is not the end, but the beginning of a new world and life with Me. Enjoy My Kingdom and My present work. Be a part of it to help bring My harvest. Do not despair.

"And you are complete in Him, which is the head of all principality and power." Colossians 2:10

... The harvest truly is plenteous, but the labourers are few; 38 Pray you therefore the Lord of the harvest, that he will send forth labourers into his harvest. Matthew 9:37-38

Dear Child,

I am the ever renewing God, the one living force behind all that is vibrantly, even slowly, changing.

You are slowly changing from moment to moment. It may require days or years for you to notice My changes. All is in My inevitable plan for the world, and you have a small role in this. Many resist My changes and cannot discern My will in them. Have no fear for the new you I desire to create. Your inner person needs constant renewal and revelation of Me to keep you joyful, thankful, maturing, and fruitful. Stay ever young in spirit.

"And He that sat upon the throne said, Behold, I make all thing new."
Revelation 21:5a

"For which cause we faint not; but though our outward man perish,
yet the inward man is renewed day by day."
II Corinthians 4:16

Dear Child,

Breathe deep of My Spirit. Stir quietly in the early sun of Spring. All the natural world is beginning to rise up. Allow your spirit to soar also above the circumstances and problems of earthly life. These will always be. But, remember Me, changeless, eternally creating the new, high above all cares. Sit with Me and gain My perspective and a greater measure of My patience, wisdom, and capacity for loving forgiveness. I offer you freedom in the middle of life's trials.

"And has raised us up together, and made us sit together
in heavenly places in Christ Jesus:" Ephesians 2:6

"If the Son therefore shall make you free, you shall be free indeed."
John 8:36

Dear Child,

I am the God who speaks. I always have words for My children. My words give them real life, continuous growth, effectiveness, and genuine progress in life. I am interested in giving them My nature, My qualities. Therefore success is available to whosoever desires it. Many despair and assume accomplishment and abundance are not available to them. This is a falsehood. I am a generous, overseeing Father who desires your fulfillment and happiness above all else. Come to Me in every need and situation.

Jesus said, "...*I am come that they might have life, and that they might have it more abundantly.*" *John 10:10*

Jesus said, "... *Whatsoever you shall ask the Father in My name. He will give it you.*" *John 16:23*

Dear Child,

I know your frame. I know you are but dust carrying My Spirit. I do not ask more of you than you can bear. These times of heat-breaking circumstances you observe with seeming little change are common to all at some time. For this, I said, come to Me in your burdens and weariness. You need reminding of your total need for and dependence on Me. It is My strength that brings you through riper and fuller in My fruit and gifts. Hold on to Me, My child. I am sufficient. In My time you will see this again.

"*For He knows our frame; He remembers that we are dust.*" *Psalm 103:14*

Jesus said, "*Come unto Me, all you that labor and are heavy laden, and I will give you rest.*" *Matthew 11:28*

Dear Child,

I am the One who holds all together and am steadfast from eternity. When your life is in My hands, you become steady, immovable, and secure. Many are the devices mankind uses to attempt security and control. They all fail in time, and I wait patiently for the turning to Me that is their only hope and salvation. Blessed are those who fail early on, and enjoy the life of surrender to Me and My Will. Enjoy My freedom and security and make it known that I am truly the way to the peace, security and joy all are seeking.

"Jesus said ..., I am the way, the truth, and the life: no man comes unto the Father, but by Me." John 14:6

"In the beginning God created the heaven and the earth." Genesis 1:1

Dear Child,

Only the humble of heart see Me in the smallest, everyday events and in creation. My hand is behind what is created and the longings of My humankind. Some seek truth in the negative influences and ramifications of life on earth—the work of your enemy. Far more fruitful is the search for Me and My laws, My power, and My purposes. I am ever at work to bring victory over all the sinful influences and outcomes. Seek Me and My eyes to truly secure understanding, knowledge, and wisdom.

Jesus said, *"Blessed are the pure in heart: for they shall see God." Matthew 5:8*

"But thanks be to God, which gives us the victory through our Lord Jesus Christ." II Corinthians 15:57

Dear Child,

My love, expressed through thoughtful kindnesses, free generosity, and wanting My best for others is pure gold in My eyes. One acquires this by surrender, painful recognition of one's own sin nature, and constant love for Me. It is available to all, and developing this love is the work of My Holy Spirit in mankind. Some, first learn of Me by the good example of others. Many must learn of Me by exposure to darkness and desiring freedom from it. Therefore, I send My laborers into the dark places to show the way to My light. I empower them with My courage and many gifts. But, My love must always go first to keep them faithful and fruitful.

Jesus said, *"This is My commandment, That you love one another, as I have loved you." John 15:12*

Jesus said, *"I am the light of the world." John 9:5*

Dear Child,

I desire you to take interest, and even joy in all that is happening around you; to be fully alive and alert. Recognize I have a purpose for all things and especially people. This is a vast idea for you, but it is true. Your role is to be steady and calm and seek to agree with Me and My purposes. This is a silent, constant prayer life, requiring focus on Me and My Word. This accomplishes much in harmony with My Spirit. It eliminates anxiety and pressure to achieve, compete, and perform. This is perfect peace.

"You will keep him in perfect peace, whose mind is stayed on You...." Isaiah 26:3

"... The effectual fervent prayer of a righteous man avails much." James 5:16b

Dear Child,

Hope is like the spring flowers, quietly waiting in times of rain, cold, and even snow. They hold steady as they were created to experience their blooming. They are designed to bring forth their life and beauty, to be what they are. So it is with you,. I designed you and your individual life to unfold by My plan. Sadly, it can be disrupted and delayed, but My hope can keep you, grow you, and overcome obstacles as you believe in Me. I am the God of purpose, saving, restoring, and reconciliation. No power is greater than mine. Place your hope afresh in Me.

"For You are my hope, O LORD God: You are my trust from my youth." Psalm 71:5

"Jesus came ..., saying, All power is given unto Me in heaven and in earth." Matthew 28:18

Dear Child,

I guard your memories and use them to illustrate My unchanging truth and love. My Spirit leads you in all the needed lessons of your life. As you reflect on the choices you make, I can reveal what is needed to seal in your memory of My ways and laws. Thereby, you grow in My wisdom and authority. You become more and more usable to Me and others. You become the head, the leader, the teacher of others. I am the God of growth and multiplication. Join Me in this joyful work.

"Howbeit when He, the Spirit of truth, is come, He will guide you into all truth...." John 16:13

"And the LORD shall make you the head, and not the tail...." Deuteronomy 28:13

Dear Child,

Many are the afflictions of those whose great desire is to walk in My righteousness. You know I will lead you out of them all, and in time to My glory. Still, I have much to accomplish through your life and hands. Take My yoke only and take My rest. Now is the time to press close to Me and be assured of My help, healing, and strength. Don't be weary in all My love-directed works. You will see unlimited fruit and harvest. Christ is gain!

"Many are the afflictions of the righteous: but the LORD delivers him out of them all." Psalm 34:19

"And let us not be weary in well doing: for in due season we shall reap, if we faint not." Galatians 6:9

Dear Child,

All is in My order as you have asked. From your side of heaven, it doesn't seem to be so. I move in the world in ways you cannot fully comprehend. The laws and words of your Bible explain enough for your to have enough faith to trust Me more and more as you grow. No one finishes growing as they walk with Me and experience My loving faithfulness. Ask for more trust and stay thankful.

"Being confident of this very thing, that He which has begun a good work in you will perform it until the day of Jesus Christ." Philippians 1:6

"In everything give thanks: for this is the will of God in Christ Jesus concerning you." I Thessalonians 5:18

Dear Child,

Trust Me, child. I am working all the experiences, relationships and events of your life into a meaningful whole. You cannot fully see it yet, but you see enough, in part, to be able to be extremely thankful. I enjoy the revelation you are receiving. Don't be hard on yourself with regrets and discouragement. All must learn through failures and correction. Many hide or deny this, but you have chosen to expose your true self for the benefit and instruction of others. This is well pleasing to Me and good use of your pain.

"I press toward the mark for the prize of the high calling of God in Christ Jesus." Philippians 3:14

"For whom the LORD loves He corrects; even as a Father the son in whom He delights." Proverbs 3:12

Peace, My Child,

Take and receive My peace. Be assured there is no need for worry or fear. Yes, there is an enemy, but I am your protective Father, the victor over all the evil of the world. Enjoy all My goodness to you under My covering wings. Make no haste. Remember how I lay My hands of blessing on My children. Allow Me to carry the cares of the world. My joy is real. My Kingdom is real. Live and be satisfied there. I smile on My children. Return My smile!

"He shall cover you with His feathers, and under His wings shall you trust: His truth shall be your shield and buckler." Psalm 91:4

"But Jesus … said, Suffer little children to come unto Me, and forbid them not: for of such is the Kingdom of God." Luke 18:16

Dear Child,

Look upon all the good I have done you and am doing you. Be of good cheer. My yoke is easy. I carry, I lead. Follow in humility, gently. I comfort and strengthen those small and weak through your presence, as a mother. Much that concerns you is of little or no importance. Receive My peace and comfort for yourself. I am with you as One who serves.

Jesus said, *"…I am among you as He that serves." Luke 22:27*

Jesus said, *"Take My yoke upon you, and learn of Me; for I am meek and lowly in heart: and you shall find rest unto your souls." Matthew 11:29*

I hear your heart, Child.

Stay thankful, trusting, with your ear attuned to Me. You ask for the gift of joy, the gift of faith. It is My Father's heart to give these gifts. What seems a mundane life, indeed is full of My purposes. Look up. See My glorious, loving handiwork and know the smallest effort for Me has great value. You are a part of My dream for the world. I want you to rejoice in it. You are mine. All My good gifts are yours!

"Follow after charity, and desire spiritual gifts…." I Corinthians 14:1

"Rejoice in the Lord always: and again I say, Rejoice." Philippians 4:4

Dear Child,

Your desire to be truly known, accepted, and loved comes from Me. I, too, long for these qualities and responses. I am a relational Father, always looking for My children to respond rightly to Me and to one another. I have made Myself clear and true consistently, and there is joy in heaven when My light dawns in a human heart. This is the beginning of new life for one who calls Me Father, and My true purposes to be fulfilled—a life of abundance.

Jesus said, *"Likewise, I say unto you, there is joy in the presence of the angels of God over one sinner that repents." Luke 15:10*

"Therefore if any man be in Christ, he is a new creature: old things have passed away; behold, all things are become new." II Corinthians 5:17

Dear Child,

I am your healer. Quiet your casting about for cures, solutions, and resolutions. Be confident that I am maintaining your life and well being by My Spirit in you. Gently follow My leading and quietly keep yourself in rest. Have I not made you and know you best? There is much that comes against you in this world, but I am your shield and buckler. Stand steady, hear My voice, and be anxious for nothing. I will provide all you need.

"...I am the LORD that heals you." Exodus 15:26d

"But my God shall supply all your need according to His riches in glory by Christ Jesus." Philippians 4:19

Dear Child,

My prophets see far ahead with Me. I have ordained them to reveal and warn. Sadly, so few hear and know what to do. In your day, much suffering could be averted if leaders could receive a wide view of consequences to all decisions. I, in justice, must allow them the reaping of what is sown. Man is ever looking, but not learning from Me and My servants. This grieves Me. I always have a good plan, a wise plan with an eye to the future.

"And the children of Issachar, which were men that had understanding of the times, to know what Israel ought to do...." I Chronicles 12:32

"Be not deceived; God is not mocked: for whatsoever a man sows, that shall he also reap." Galatians 6:7

Yes, My Child,

The pressures and possibilities from without cause you to desire relief from My narrow path. In these times, you can trust that I know and understand your need for refreshing and a change of place. Also, trust that I can and will provide this in My way and time. Seek Me and not an escape. My path always leads to what grows My life in you. There will be fresh, green pastures for you. Let Me direct your feet in righteousness, hold fast, wait on Me. and see My hand of provision as you serve me. I do all things well.

Jesus said, "Because straight is the gate, and narrow is the way, which leads unto life, and few there be that find it." Matthew 7:14

*"He makes me to lie down in green pastures:
He leads me beside the still waters. He restores my soul:
He leads me in the paths of righteousness for His Name's sake."
Psalm 23:2-3*

Dear Child,

I hear your confessions of sins. I cleanse and forgive them. I understand your frailty. Keep watch over your tongue. All thoughts and feelings need to come under My Spirit's captivity. Expressing only those that I reveal will truly bring life to you and others. Live in your Spirit so as not to be deceived by passing feelings and easy, surface ideas, and opinions. Let deep call unto deep. Draw waters of life from My wells of salvation.

"A wholesome tongue is a tree of life...." Proverbs 15:4a

"Casting down imaginations, and
every high thing that exalts itself against the knowledge of God,
and bringing into captivity every thought to the obedience of Christ."
II Corinthians 10:5

Dear Child,

Yes, faith grows, and I desire it to grow and do wonders. Your faith affects others and causes them to consider who I am. It pleases Me to know your certain, sure dependence on Me and your unwavering expectation of My unfailing goodness. Relationship, living, active, creative is what I desire, not perfection. To see you grow through all your life experiences and seasons is My Father's heart's desire.

"Now faith is the substance of things hoped for,
the evidence of things not seen." Hebrews 11:1

"Surely goodness and mercy shall follow me all the days of my life:
and I will dwell in the house of the LORD for ever."
Psalm 23:6

Dear Child,

Stay conscious of Me as a Friend that sticks closer than a brother. In this way, you will expect less from others and be calm in the face of disappointments. Within you and all around you, I am moving, creating, unfolding My miraculous, supernatural power. When you are choosing Me, moment by moment, you truly experience the wonder, joy, and reality of My Kingdom. That is enough; My sufficiency.

"For in Him we live, and move, and have our being...." Acts 17:28a

"Not that we are sufficient of ourselves to think anything as of ourselves; but our sufficiency is of God;" II Corinthians 3:5

Dear Child,

I have, I am and I will extend My care for you. No weapon formed against you shall prosper. I have your life plan and destiny in mind. I called you to teach, to heal, and to go, and I have not finished My work through you. Refrain from fear and dark thoughts. I bring light; I am light and My light fills you and your life. Rejoice and be glad. You are mine. None can harm you.

"Casting all your care upon Him; for He cares for you." I Peter 5:7

"For you were sometimes darkness, but now are you light in the Lord: walk as children of light:" Ephesians 5:8

Dear Child,

Yes, My Spirit leads you in all truth. This means continuous revelation of My creative capacity that knows no limits. I use your life experiences to show you the reality of My ways and My unchanging Kingdom where all is perfection. You recognize patterns in events, lives, generations, and people that reveal My invisible principles, laws, and Hand. How rich I make you when all you see is Me and My motive of love for the world.

"Jesus said unto him, I am the way, the truth, and the life: no man comes to the Father, but by Me." John 14:6

"For God so loved the world, that He gave His only begotten Son, that whosoever believes in Him should not perish, but have everlasting life." John 3:16

Dear Child,

Planting, growing, multiplying—these are My interests, in which I interest and instruct My people. I desire the maximum use of resources as a gardener, looking after My Kingdom. I put this interest and passion in hearts willing to hear, obey, go. I look on the earth and mankind as My glorious, special project of growth towards Me. Choose to work with My Spirit of truth to see flourishing on earth, of that which is visible and that which is invisible. I lavish My love upon the earth as a generous, wealthy Father, the Great Gardener.

"For the LORD shall comfort Zion: He will comfort all her waste places; and He will make her wilderness like Eden, and her desert like the garden of the LORD; joy and gladness shall be found therein, thanksgiving, and the voice of melody." Isaiah 51:3

"For by Him were all things created, that are in heaven, and that are in earth, visible and invisible, whether they be thrones, or dominions, or principalities, or powers: all things were created by Him and for Him." Colossians 1:16

Dear Child,

Yes, attune your heart and inner ears to My still, quiet voice as you move through your life activity. Even as you sleep, you can hear Me and receive revelation from My Spirit. Stay close to Me, letting the foolish trends of the world pass by, not affecting you. There is a glory in seeing Me and My ways and Kingdom all around you that satisfies above all else. Eternal pleasure and delight are Mine to give. Receive as from My loving hand.

Jesus said, *"Who has ears to hear, let him hear." Matthew 11:15*

"You will show me the path of life: in Your presence: is fullness of joy; at Your right hand there are pleasures for evermore." Psalm 16:11

Dear Child,

Freedom from worry and cares that hinder is My gift to My children. I release you to joyful security, as My family on earth. I cover you with My wings of protection and favor. Much happens in the unseen realm where I oversee, send help, arrange events, and work miracles. All this is incomprehensible to you but very real. Listen intently to My voice and heed My revelations, so you can make decisions and adjustments in agreement and harmony with Me. Delight to do My will.

"Let us therefore come boldly unto the throne of grace, that we may obtain mercy, and find grace to help in time of need." Hebrews 4:16

"I delight to do Your Will, O My God: yes, Your Law is within my heart." Psalm 40:8 (Capitals are the author's)

Dear Child,

All the good gifts are from Me. During My time on the cross and in the grave, I took control of all evil and made available all the good. Nothing was overlooked. My desire is for My children to recognize and receive all of this from My loving Hand. The simplicity of receiving should be clear. Whosoever will may come and receive. I delight to give and give more. In this season of considering Me and My offer of salvation, rejoice in My overwhelming generosity and overflowing love.

"Every good gift and every perfect gift is from above, and comes down from the Father of lights, with whom is no variableness, neither shadow of turning." James 1:17

Jesus said, *"I have glorified You on the earth: I have finished the work which You gave Me to do." John 17:4*

Dear Child,

I have spoken through My prophets, and today I make this gift available to all., to whosoever seeks to know My will. I give dreams and visions to the humble, sincere ones. I would not have you shocked, nor unprepared at what must happen before My return to earth. Keep pace with My Spirit, pouring out, that all may take the opportunity to know Me. These times are ordained by My Father to bring all earthly things to a just conclusion. We do all things well and perfectly timed. My loving wisdom makes understanding a possibility and comfort to My chosen children.

"And it shall come to pass in the last days, says God, I will pour out of My Spirit upon all flesh: and your sons and your daughters shall prophesy, and your young men shall see visions, and your old men shall dream dreams: 18 And on My servants and on My handmaidens I will pour out in those days of My Spirit; and they shall prophesy." Acts 2:17-18

Jesus said, *"And you shall know the truth, and the truth shall make you free." John 8:32*

Spring around Easter

Dear Child,

Because I rose, you shall also rise. This is My gift of love, great love, to all mankind. Be at peace in this security I have purchased for you. Yes, My blood is precious beyond words, even a mystery. Its power is also eternal. It works continuous miracles, transformations, and brings meaning to human life. Avail yourself of My most precious blood purchased relationship gifts—salvation, restoration, healing, and reconciliation. It is My complete work; available to all mankind.

Jesus said, *"For this is My blood of the new testament, which is shed for many for the remission of sins."* Matthew 26:28

"And that He was buried, and that He rose again the third day according to the scriptures:" 1 Corinthians 15:4

Dear Child,

All that you are, can be, and have is from Me. Few can see that I am all you need. I provide the close, intimate understanding, belonging, security, protection, and care that you, as a tender plant, need. Man has the illusion that all this comes from him, but I am the true source. My Kingdom causes all life to flow and be maintained in balance. Often, it is the deceived work of man that causes the imbalance, trouble, and disasters on earth. I am always the faithful, merciful, forbearing, healing Redeemer, Restorer, and Keeper.

"But My God shall supply all your need according to His riches in glory by Christ Jesus." Philippians 4:19

"He restores my soul: He leads me in the paths of righteousness for His Name's sake." Psalm 23:3

Dear Child,

Yes, these are the days of Elijah, prophesied at the close of time. There is talk of peace, but only My children rest in My peace. Great anxiety covers the nations standing against one another. My solutions, My laws, and My order are ignored, denied, and not believed. This grieves Me. However, My joy is in those who press on, serving and believing, in the midst of the darkness, lawlessness, and confusion. Truly, they are the light of the world for Me.

*"And Jesus answered, Elijah truly shall first come,
and restore all things." Matthew 17:11*

*Jesus said, "I am come a light into the world,
that whosoever believes on Me should not abide in darkness.
John 12:46*

Dear Child,

Rest, allow My joy to take over. Yes, I correct you, then forgive as you rededicate yourself to My will. Then, be released from all self-blame. I am your ever-present Father. I will not abandon you or distance Myself from you. We are now united again in a sort of dance. Dancing is a joy response from Me to you and from you back to Me. Observe the laughter of children. It just is. Be and rest in that present security.

*"Rest in the LORD, and wait patiently for Him: fret not yourself
because of him who prospers in his way, because of the man
who brings wicked devices to pass." Psalm 37:7*

"You have turned for me my mourning into dancing...." Psalm 30:11

"A merry heart does good like a medicine...." Proverbs 17:22a

Dear Child,

Remember, I am the One who transforms, reveals Myself, and changes people and circumstances. Your role is assistant and cooperator. Look to Me first, not to what you want to change. Examine yourself, care for what needs to change in yourself. Many complications occur when you attempt to change another person according to your ideas and methods. Allow My oil of joy to soothe you and smooth your relationships. Extend grace, acceptance, and peace. In this atmosphere, I can and will work transformations in My right way and timing.

"And be not conformed to this world: but be you transformed by the renewing of your mind, that you may prove what is that good, and acceptable, and perfect will of God." Romans 12:2

"For we are laborers together with God: you are God's husbandry, you are God's building." I Corinthians 3:9

Dear Child,

I build Myself and My way into the secure life foundations of those who believe. Nothing else holds steady in the high winds coming upon the earth. My order and answers are available in earth's chaos and seeming impossibilities. For those who believe in Me, there is meaning and purpose in life on earth, as well as secure hope for eternal life. Turning your soul and face towards Me, the "Sun of Righteousness," eases the pain that cannot be avoided on earth. I am larger than you can imagine. My love extends to all people.

Jesus said, *"Therefore, whosoever hears these sayings of Mine, and does them, I will liken him to a wise man, which built his house upon a rock: 25 And the rain descended, and the floods came, and the winds blew, and beat upon that house; and it fell not: for it was founded upon a rock." Matthew 7:24-25*

"But unto you that fear My Name shall the Sun of Righteousness arise with healing in His wings; and you shall go forth, and grow up as calves of the stall." Malachi 4:2

Dear Child,

I call, equip, gift, and ordain. This I see in My wise plan. Some agree, co-operate, co-labor, learn, and flourish. This is entirely your choice. I have no limitations and hindrances to what I do. Have no concern about My plans and provisions, wherever I send you. Seemingly mundane service has great power and influence when done in love under My direction. Simplicity is the quality I use best. It is My Spirit in you that works the wonders. Enjoy the experience. It is My gift to My children.

Jesus said, "You have not chosen Me, but I have chosen you, and ordained you, that you should go and bring forth fruit, and that your fruit should remain: that whatsoever you shall ask of the Father in My Name, He may give it you." John 15:16

"...Not by might, nor by power, but by My Spirit, says the LORD of hosts." Zechariah 4:6a

Dear Child,

I am a gentle, persistent, all-knowing Father. I know when you are ready to grow into more maturity and depth of intimacy with Me; when you willingly want to recognize a new level of dying to your self-life. I don't force the leaves to appear or the rose to open. So it is with your inner life. The light of My countenance and the warmth of My love draw up waters of loving acceptance in you. Sweet revelation of Me causes your heart to desire the true, vivid life that's only found in Me. All else becomes pale shadows of what is real, and will no longer satisfy you. This is eternal, lovely springtime with Me.

"The LORD make His face shine upon you, and be gracious unto you: 26 The LORD lift up His countenance upon you, and give you peace." Numbers 6:25-26

Jesus said, "And this is life eternal, that they might know You the only true God, and Jesus Christ whom You have sent." John 17:3

Dear Child,

I too grew weary as a man walking on earth. There is no condemnation for your human weakness and limitations. I drew strength and comfort from family and friends. I learned to take rest and nourishment as My Father led and provided. I also showed you how to draw away at times to quiet and solitary places. All was, and still is, made available to My children. Receive fully and give freely as My way is making you a strong source and model of faithful, balanced obedience and generosity. Your weakness showcases My victorious strength.

"There is therefore now no condemnation to them which are in Christ Jesus, who walk not after the flesh, but after the Spirit." Roman 8:1

"And in the morning, rising up a great while before day, He went out, and departed into a solitary place, and there prayed." Mark 1:35

Dear Child,

Truly, you are wonderfully, even awesomely created. My intention is for you to recognize Me, your Creator, in the extraordinary functioning of your body and its interconnectedness with your soul, and ultimately with your spirit. Recognize how I have thought of all the needed functions and repairs of your body. How useful and pleasant are the possible ways you can act; how miraculously you can multiply. I have made Myself known in your complete being. None can say I am unknowable.

"I will praise You; for I am fearfully and wonderfully made: marvelous are Your works; and that my soul knows right well." Psalm 139:14

"For in Him dwells all the fullness of the Godhead bodily. 10 And you are complete in Him, which is the Head of all principalities and power." Colossians 2:9-10

Dear Child,

I am in the transformation work. I take the natural, often raw, human material, and radiate it with My Spirit. This Truth illumination causes the mind and nervous system to be changed. Therefore, the values, desires, goals, and dreams come into line and agreement with mine. I bring a new security, calm and vision where there was chaos, unfulfillment and lack of purpose. I do the same healing and restoration to the extent of your faith in and dependence on Me and My ways. I want a complete work and overflowing life for My children.

"And be not conformed to this world: but be you transformed by the renewing of your mind, that you may prove what is that good, and acceptable, and perfect, will of God." Romans 12:2

"And I will restore to you the years that the locust has eaten...." Joel 2:25a

Dear Child,

Mothering is My idea of fulfillment—filling hearts full of peace and gratitude. Bringing forth life is My planned way to a new place of honor and revelation to those who receive a child from Me. I have good intentions for every life, even in what might appear to be impossible circumstances and pain. Pain is often needed for one to turn their attention to Me. Sorrow turns to joy for those who want to be givers of life to others. I am their hope anchor.

*"So God created man in His own image, in the image of God created He him; male and female created He them. 28 And God blessed them, and God said unto them, Be fruitful and multiply...."
Genesis 1:27-28a*

"Which hope we have as an anchor of the soul...." Hebrews 6:19a

Dear Child,

Be comforted. I understand the anguish of your heart over your weak, sinful nature. I see the many pressures coming against you in your natural life. You experience some of My pain over the flagrant rebellion and darkness of sin in the world. But, be assured, I am the Father, close by you who always forgives your weeping, repentant confession. Now, look up and be of good cheer; be My handmaiden to many. A harvest is ahead. I am with you.

"He that covers his sins shall not prosper: but whoso confesses and forsakes them shall have mercy." Proverbs 28:13

"And on My servants and on My handmaidens I will pour out in those days of My Spirit; and they shall prophesy:" Acts 2:18

Dear Child,

Allow lesser concerns to fall away as I call you to My greater concerns. Agree with Me for My outcomes in the great needs, conflicts, and misunderstandings happening on earth. As nations threaten to rise up against nations, and fires of war blot out My purposes, stand in prayer for My ultimate outcomes: good out of evil. Share My grief at the loss and great pain man causes against man. Hope in the day when My Kingdom comes, to end man's sinful deceptions and hatreds. Find nurture and peace in My revealed, loving goodness to you today and each day. Trust all to Me your caring Father.

Jesus said, *"But when you shall hear of wars and commotions, be not terrified: for these things must first come to pass; but the end is not by and by. 10 Then said He unto them, Nation shall rise against nation, and kingdom against kingdom:" Luke 21:9-10*

"... The effectual fervent prayer of a righteous man avails much." James 5:16b

Dear Child,

Waiting and watching are a part of My ways. Together, we are effective in My will being done. I grieve and you grieve for the great sorrows of mankind and the cruelty of the enemy of My people. This evil is ongoing until I return and halt the power to destroy. I am with you to help you grow and flourish in the knowledge of Me. I am your comfort and peace as you watch, wait, and pray. My blood can always atone for the repentant. Take hope, and cheer yourself in My promises that never change. Sorrow only lasts through the night, but My joy comes in the morning.

Jesus said, *"...watch and pray:*
for you know not when the time is." Mark 13:33

Jesus said, *"I came not to call the righteous,*
but sinners to repentance." Luke 5:32

Dear Child,

There is My true peace that can be experienced in all circumstances. There is much fear in your world on earth. It has become part of the unconscious thinking of man without his knowing. Only faith in Me, and knowing Me in worship and revelation can drive away this culture of fear. Be one who is courageous in faith to walk in My true peace and confidence. I still rule and reign, and I shepherd My flock through danger and threat. Remain under My rod and My staff, close to Me and close to those who love Me too. Be of good courage.

"You will keep him in perfect peace, whose mind is stayed on You:
because he trusts in You." Isaiah 26:3

"...I will fear no evil: for You are with me;
Your rod and Your staff they comfort me." Psalm 23:4

Dear Child,

Listen. Listen and learn of Me. Recognize My voice and My works and wonders. Many go through life on the surface, not truly seeing and understanding that they are My creation and are surrounded by My creation and by all that I continue to create. Therefore, I call teachers and preachers to awaken My people. I awaken, teach, and reveal, so that much can be passed on and extended to many more. There are no limits to My reach to all mankind. This is My plan and it shall be accomplished. Hear My voice; hear My call.

Jesus said, "My sheep hear My voice, and I know them, and they follow Me:" John 10:27

"And He gave some, apostles; and some, prophets; and some, evangelists; and some, pastors and teachers; 12 For the perfecting of the saints, for the work of the ministry, for the edifying of the body of Christ" Ephesians 4:11-12

Dear Child,

Looking to the left and right is not the answer to your trouble. Hold steady in Me, pleasing Me. There is no hope in the goal of pleasing others at My expense. Consider My faithful leadership through many years, and know it will not change. As always, be a good, close follower, a ready learner, and servant. I am your glory and lifter of your head. Much of life on earth involves the mundane. See My glory in all. Look on Me.

"For I am the LORD, I change not...." Malachi 3:6a

"But you, O LORD, are a shield for me; my glory, and the lifter up of mine head." Psalm 3:3

Dear Child,

As I have set before you a call to go in My Name, I have also given you My power and strength to fulfill all I have in mind. Your thinking of all that could go wrong is not My thinking. Set your mind on Me and on the good that can be accomplished as I set your plan in motion. I have intentions to delight you as you see Me in many new places and faces. I also know your need for refreshing and rejuvenation. Am I not your good Father of lavish giving?

"And Jesus came ... saying, All power is given unto Me in heaven and in earth. Go you therefore, and teach all nations, baptizing them in the Name of the Father, and of the Son, and of the Holy Spirit."
Matthew 28:18-19

"Set your affection on things above, not on things on the earth."
Colossians 3:2

Dear Child,

My face is shining upon you, for I am pleased as you respond with a yes to My leading. Remember My faithfulness. I do not send you alone. I will radiate My love through you as I reveal Myself to many. As I said, some plant, some water, some harvest, and some encourage the harvesters with joy and thankfulness. Be glad for labor to fulfill. All My resources are at your hand; give liberally as I say. Your eyes and ears will see and hear Me wherever you go; as I go before you always. Have My mind and My heart as you go. See the wonders I am doing and rejoice.

"The LORD make His face shine upon you, and be gracious unto you." *Number 6:25*

"Now he that plants and he that waters are one: and every man shall receive his own reward according to his own labor. 9 For we are laborer together with God: you are God's husbandry, you are God's building." *I Corinthians 3:8-9*

Dear Child,

Trees do not question what they are. They just adjust to their surroundings as they slowly become what they are to be. So, too, you are planted like a tree by My pure, ever-flowing water. Day by day, night by night, you are becoming what you are to be under My shepherding. Trust My wise purposes and presence. I see the real you; the one I intended from the beginning, complete, fulfilled, satisfied. I am your Creator!

"But his delight is in the law of the LORD; and in His law does he meditate day and night. 3 And he shall be like a tree planted by the rivers of water, that brings forth his fruit in his season; his leaf also shall not wither; and whatsoever he does shall prosper." Psalm 1:2-3

"The LORD is my shepherd; I shall not want." Psalm 23:1

Dear Child,

Vanity, pleasing others, desiring the praise of others cannot be your heart's desire. My desire is that your soul will flourish according to your individual destiny. For this, you need Me as your first desire. All men need Me, yet, in reality, so few find Me. The restless seeking and pursuits of mankind are rooted in their need to know Me and their value to Me. For this reason, I say go, tell, share, give help that I might be made known to every person. Through this sending, I make Myself known in ways that cannot be denied. I am the Savior, saving, healing, restoring whosoever will receive Me.

"If we live in the Spirit, let us also walk in the Spirit. 26 Let us not be desiring of vain glory, provoking one another, envying one another." Galatians 5:25-26

"Delight yourself also in the LORD; and He shall give you the desires of your heart. 5 Commit your way unto the LORD; trust also in Him; and He shall bring it to pass." Psalm 37:4-5

Dear Child,

There is much in your world you would like to change and fix. However, I am the only lasting fix. Nothing you plan or work on will remain fixed. All is in constant change according to My overseeing plan. Fix your eyes on Me. Work with Me. Follow Me. Agree with Me. Enjoy Me. Ask of Me. I make plans succeed in My way and time. I make goodness and mercy follow you. Have no concern for the outcomes of any matter on earth. My truth stands and always will prevail in the end. Stand with Me.

"O God, my heart is fixed;
I will sing and give praise, even with my glory." Psalm 108:1

"Thus says the LORD, the Holy One of Israel, and his Maker,
Ask Me of things to come concerning My sons, and
concerning the work of My hands command you Me."
Isaiah 45:11

Dear Child,

My yoke is easy. Therefore, you can release yourself to follow after Me in your daily challenges. Calmly, orderly, as you go in full consciousness of My presence and Divine enabling, all will be accomplished. Remember, all you have is now, today, in My Kingdom. Keep too much emphasis on the past or future out of your thoughts unless I bring it to you for My good teaching purposes. Experience every small detail of My activity and work. I intend to delight and surprise you continually. These pleasures are at My right hand and cause all earthly ones to come into the correct perspective. Serve me with gladness and ease.

"…at Your right hand there are pleasures for evermore." Psalm 16:11b

"Serve the LORD with gladness;
come before His presence with singing." Psalm 100:2

Dear Child,

Yes, I am a man of sorrows and acquainted with grief. As you walk and grow with me, you also experience My sorrows and grief. This is inevitable. But, I also give you revelation of My answers, hope, and joy after sorrow. So, be pleased to pass on My answers and hope that many receive My gracious salvation, ultimate understanding and joy. I have overcome all the sorrows of the world and open the door for all to also be overcomers, that your joy may be full.

"He is despised and rejected of men; a man of sorrows, and acquainted with grief...." Isaiah 53:3a

Jesus said, "... In the world you shall have tribulation: but be of good cheer; I have overcome the world." John 16:33b

Dear Child,

Well used experiences ought to make you a well-used channel of My life in its endless forms. All the varied ways of expressing My love and Gospel will carry you through life's seasons with awe and blessings. Be willing to obey and empty yourself to make room for the ever-flowing new. Do not be stagnant nor grudging. My Spirit will keep you awake, generous, and fruitful. You can be youthful without worry at any season of life. In eternity, everything is always new.

"Let all the earth fear the LORD: let all the inhabitants of the world stand in awe of Him." Psalm 33:8

"Those that be planted in the house of the LORD shall flourish in the courts of our God. 14 They shall bring forth fruit in old age; they shall be fat and flourishing." Psalm 92:13-14

Dear Child,

The exquisite construction of the flowers and plants you see and handle, speak of Me and My perfection. Formed on earth, they reflect My thoughts, infinite in variety and placement. Their intricate details and fragrances speak of My desire to delight and be of use. How much greater was My perfect thought when I created you, mankind. It was for My pleasure and usefulness also. Each one must discover their place, value, and purpose through Me their Creator. Only then can true fulfillment, satisfaction, and joy be experienced.

"He is the Rock, His work is perfect: for all His ways are judgment: a God of truth and without iniquity, just and right is He."
Deuteronomy 32:4

"Even every one that is called by my name: for I have created him for my glory...." Isaiah 43:7 -

Dear Child,

For many, this is a season of new beginnings. Farmers plant, lovers marry, students graduate. In all this anticipation, is My desire to grow things. My heart is to bring My people to new heights of understanding Me. I also want them to grow in their understanding of themselves and of what true fruitfulness is. Man usually sees only the outer manifestations of My desires and assumes it is his own work.. For those closest to Me, there is a certain responsibility to not only recognize My hands, always at work but to also make Me known to those who walk in deception and darkness. It has always been so.

And that he might make known the riches of his glory on the vessels of mercy, which he had afore prepared unto glory, Romans 9:23

"While we look not at the things which are seen, but at the things which are not seen: for the things which are seen are temporal; but the things which are not seen are eternal." II Corinthians 4:18

Dear Child,

I said come to Me when you're tired and burdened because I know this will be the case sometimes. There's no shame in your human limitations. I created you for a balance in all things. Sometimes, you must learn and choose balance through hard circumstances. I come to you most clearly in your times of weakness and need. I speak to you of rest, surrender, and letting go. These are all essential to your life with Me and maturity. Prayer is not just petition and asking. It is deep quiet with Me where words from you are not always needed. You may weep on your Father's breast.

"Surely I have behaved and quieted myself as a child that is weaned of his mother: my soul is even as a weaned child." Psalm 131:2

"... Blessed are you that weep now: for you shall laugh." Luke 6:21b

Dear Child,

Yes, when you turn your thoughts to My immense universe, as well as My smallest benefits to man, you can worship no other. You can know Me as Savior and Friend, yet in My magnitude, you cannot grasp Me fully. Therefore, you can look past the many, endless needs and problems of life on earth, knowing there is a great, glorious eternity ahead for those who believe in and love Me. This brings comfort and a peaceful perspective to My dear children and pleases Me, their Father.

"O come, let us worship and bow down: let us kneel before the LORD our Maker." Psalm 95:6

"For the LORD takes pleasure in His people: He will beautify the meek with salvation." Psalm 149:4

Dear Child,

There is the voice of one who accuses. You must run from this voice; rebuke it and refuse to listen. My correction is kind, showing what I desire for your ultimate well being. Remember, those who do not follow and love Me, follow another, whether they recognize it or not. There are many idols available; the most common one is self. Continue to keep your focus on Me and what I say. I cover you in the storms of confusion, fear, and sorrow. I am your comfort and keeper. Believe Me and be well.

*"Submit yourselves therefore to God.
Resist the devil, and he will flee from you." James 4:7*

"And I heard a loud voice saying in heaven, Now is come salvation, and strength, and the kingdom of our God, and the power of His Christ: for the accuser of our brethren is cast down, which accused them before our God day and night." Revelation 12;10

Dear Child,

As My servant, your ears need to be attuned to My requests and directions. This requires not only your availability and obedience but most importantly, a clean heart and a spirit rightly related to Me. Do not be surprised when I convict or correct you as needed. I cannot allow you to be deceived about your own sins and motives. These must be cleaned and taken responsibility for. I am always working a gentle, quiet spirit in you, with less need to speak and more to listen. Your self may not find this pleasant, but self needs to die.

*"Create in me a clean heart, O God; and renew a right spirit within me."
Psalm 51:10*

"Wherefore, my beloved brethren, let every man be swift to hear, slow to speak, slow to wrath:" James 1:19

Dear Child,

I am the Heavenly Bridegroom awaiting My earthly Bride for an eternal union only I can conceive of. My Bride, the Church, that has grown on earth to truly know and adore Me, is also waiting and preparing. The preparations have taken thousands of years, but to Me, this is as days. Much had to be done and revealed as mankind was able to understand and receive. I am a patient Father, and My work is thorough and enduring. My Bride is precious and dazzling to Me. She longs for Me and shall not be disappointed. I invite, Come to the Lamb's wedding.

"But, beloved, be not ignorant of this one thing, that one day is with the Lord as a thousand years, and a thousand years as one day." II Peter 3:8

"Let us be glad and rejoice, and give honor to Him: for the marriage of the Lamb has come, and His wife has made herself ready.' Revelation 19:7

Dear Child,

Repentance is My love gift to My wayward children. Sin occurs in many subtle ways, often unrecognized until My Spirit reveals it by way of conviction. Underlying sinful behavior and thoughts are the deeper depths of potential depravity and destruction. Often, these break forth in one's life unexpectedly and suddenly. These are opportunities for great transformation through genuine repentance and self-awareness. I provide all that is needed for truth in the inward parts. Receive all I desire to give and find true life.

"...the goodness of God leads you to repentance...." Romans 2:4

"Behold, You desire truth in the inward parts: and in the hidden part You shall make me to know wisdom." Psalm 51:6

Dear Child,

To see My face, to draw close to Me in the early hours of the day is a gift few experience. To feel My loving acceptance is warmth to your heart, strength to your body, and protection for today. You needn't explain all the complications of life on earth. Leave them for a time to rest on Me. I feel the pain and weaknesses of My people and send all that you need to overcome them. Receive and be comforted, moment by moment, waiting and resting on Me. I know how much you can bear, and then, I am your release, refuge, and restoration. I take your burdens.

"When You said, Seek you My face; my heart said unto You, Your face, LORD, will I seek." Psalm 27:8

"God is our refuge and strength, a very present help in trouble." Psalm 46:1

My Dear Child,

Desperation and hopelessness can press a person to extremes and foolishness, especially for those who do not know Me as their Father of love and hope. I am always waiting with the answer and with outstretched arms in the place of hope for every human need. For this, I have called My servants to act, and to write My words for safekeeping. I hear the calls and cries of those even who do not yet know Me. Hold fast to Me, encourage yourself and others to look to Me and My words with secure hope, waiting for My reply. There is no other God, Creator, and Father other than Me, Jesus of Nazareth, whose Spirit is available to all on earth. Go in expectation of My goodness.

"Hear my prayer, O LORD, give ear to my supplications: in Your faithfulness answer me, and in Your righteousness." Psalm 143:1

"But to us there is but one God, the Father, of whom are all things, and we in Him; and one Lord Jesus Christ, by whom are all things, and we by Him." I Corinthians 8:6

My Dear Child,

There are many afflictions that come to the righteous due to living in the midst of much sorrow and confusion. But I am not the source of these wrongs. I prove Myself as your loving Father who brings you out of these troubles, wiser, and more dependent on Me. Weep freely in times of sadness and pain, for afterward there will come laughter in greater measure. Learn to come to Me when you are heavy laden, knowing I will surely give you rest. Blessed and happy are you when you are hungry and needy of Me.

"Many are the afflictions of the righteous: but the LORD delivers him out of them all." Psalm 34:19

Jesus said, "Blessed are they which do hunger and thirst after righteousness; for they shall be filled." Matthew 5:6

Dear Child,

My mercy is so vast, you cannot fully comprehend My ways with My children. My Spirit is unseen as it protects and leads My little ones away from danger and loss. I cover you from much that is unnecessary to your growth. As you grow in the knowledge of Me through the years, I renew your youth and cause great rejoicing in you. As you wait upon Me and do not rush in or move without My wise guidance, I cause you to rise up on eagle's wings, above the cares of life. Heavenly realms are My reward to those who look to Me in trust.

"I will greatly rejoice in the LORD, my soul shall be joyful in my God; for He has clothed me with the garments of salvation, He has covered me with the robe of righteousness, as a bridegroom decks himself with ornaments, and as a bride adorns herself with her jewels." Isaiah 61:10

"Bless the LORD, O my soul, and forget not all His benefits: 3 Who forgives all your iniquities; who heals all your diseases; 4 Who redeems your life from destruction; who crowns you with loving kindness and tender mercies; 5 Who satisfies your mouth with good things; so that your youth is renewed like the eagle's." Psalm 103:2-5

Dear Child,

Yes, I am the God of all generations. Just as you see the natural world renewing itself and multiplying in kind, so I have designed the human realm. I have built into you the reservoir of human experience as you come from your parents and all the past parents on earth. This is a great mystery that cannot be fully fathomed by you. Nevertheless, it is a source of inspiration, motivation, giftings and My grace to you. Gratitude and humility should go before you as you invest now in the generations to follow you and Me.

"For the LORD is good; His mercy is everlasting;
and His truth endures to all generations." Psalm 100:5

"So God created man in His own image, in the image of God created
He him; male and female created He them. 28 And God blessed them,
and said unto them, Be fruitful, and multiply, and replenish the earth"
Genesis 1:27-28

My Dear Child,

Practice My peaceful Presence, and allow Me to turn away all anxiety. I bring others to your attention and thoughts so that you may agree with Me for their best. I may reveal what is needed in support or actions. Usually, just agreeing with Me is enough. Bringing additional responsibility on yourself is not needed, and can cause anxiety or fear. You are able to recognize this and bring your every thought captive to Me. Remember, the government is upon My shoulder, not yours.

"(For the weapons of our warfare are not carnal, but mighty through
God to the pulling down of strong holds.) 5 Casting down imaginations,
and every high thing that exalts itself against the knowledge of God, and
bringing into captivity every thought to the obedience of Christ."
II Corinthians 10:4-5

"For unto us a child is born, unto us a Son is given: and the government
shall be upon His shoulder...." Isaiah 9:6a

Dear Child,

When I say, guard your heart with all diligence, I mean for you to keep your focus on your inner life with Me. The world is full of distractions, interruptions, and pains you might be tempted to focus on. These can be the source of many wrong reactions. It is My desire for you to keep your real inner self calm and teachable so that My Spirit is leading and responding through you. This process requires your willingness to be trained in righteousness, obedient to My truth; indeed, a life long learning to trust and love Me as the trustworthy Father I am.

"Keep your heart with all diligence; for out of it are the issues of life."
Proverbs 4:23

"Howbeit, when He, the Spirit of truth, is come,
He will guide you into all truth...."
John 16:13a

Dearest Child,

Can you feel My love today? I am refreshing you as the spring rains fall. I am ever-present, but today you feel Me in a wave of My peace. I never change and am always available to hold you by My right, secure hand. Fill your mind and heart with My deep Word, and refuse the world's ever-changing bad news. The simplicity of My eternal good news is more than enough for all the world. Today, as you contemplate My crucifixion, rejoice and be glad in My goodness that is boundless and beautiful.

"You have given me the shield of Your salvation: and Your right hand has held me up, and Your gentleness has made me great." *Psalm 18:35*

"Oh how great is Your goodness,
which you have laid up for them that fear You:
which You have wrought for them that trust in You
before the sons of men!" *Psalm 31:19*

Dear Child,

Yes, profound, beyond words is My exchange made for mankind. Only those who recognize their separation from Me can deeply rejoice in My way of reconciliation. There is a security I give to those who come home to Me in confession of personal sin and need. They find their place in Me as a child, accepted and belonging. All have not only sinned themselves, but the need goes deeper. A recognition of the human potential for all sin and evil causes the true heart cry for Me. I am the only way, truth, and life given for all mankind's real needs.

"Therefore if any man be in Christ, he is a new creature: old things are passed away; behold, all things are become new. 18 And all things are of God, who has reconciled us to Himself by Jesus Christ, and has given to us the ministry of reconciliation;" II Corinthians 5:17-18

"I cried unto the LORD with my voice; with my voice unto the LORD did I make my supplication. 2 I poured out my complaint before Him; I showed before Him my trouble." Psalm 142:1-2

Dear Child,

Yes, My grace is truly sufficient for all your needs on earth. I have provided the way of inner peace that brings outer peace. With My grace as your example, you can have grace for yourself and others. You can suffer long with others, be kind, and truthful. As I heal your needy and broken places, you can see the same in others and respond accordingly and lovingly. As always, I am growing a fruitful life in and through you. Do not reject the pain that leads to My real righteousness in you.

Jesus said, *"My grace is sufficient for you: for My strength is made perfect in weakness." Most gladly therefore will I rather glory in my infirmities, that the power of Christ may rest upon me." II Corinthians 12:9*

"He heals the broken in heart, and binds up their wounds." Psalm 147:3

Dearest Child,

It pleases Me when I can astonish you with some completely new revelation of Myself. When you are drawn to consider the immense, diverse creation of the earth, and what you can know of its history and purpose, you catch a brief glimpse of Me and your small place in My creation. You see how much value I place on every human life, and how little I am understood. All these thoughts baffle you, and bring you to a deeper humility, worship and wonder. Yes, I am pleased by the time and consideration you give Me. You desire to lean on Me, and depend on Me, and love Me more.

"The earth is the LORD's, and the fullness thereof; the world, and they that dwell therein." Psalm 24:1

"For You are great, and do wondrous things: You are God alone." Psalm 86:10

Dear Child,

Concerning what is termed Easter: Much of the world may turn away from the horror of My crucifixion. But, you, My dear children, can see only the beauty and unspeakable love poured out in My blood, powerful enough to cleanse every sin. Rejoice in Me as never before. I am close to you and well pleased.

Paul said, "I am crucified with Christ: nevertheless I live; yet not I, but Christ lives in me: and the life which I now live in the flesh I live by the faith of the Son of God, who loved me, and gave Himself for me." Galatians 2:20

"But if we walk in the light, as He is in the light, we have fellowship one with another, and the blood of Jesus Christ His Son cleanses us from all sin." I John 1:7

Dear One,

Preparing My Bride is a way of expressing My plan for My people, My church. Laying up those qualities, character and virtues needed, is another way of saying preparations are being made. All this takes time to develop, as My Spirit is given out in waves of power and revelation. Your response is to receive, recognize, be cleansed and become Mine alone. This preparation is available to all who will choose Me as Bridegroom, grooming My Bride for eternity and My marriage supper.

"He that has the Bride is the Bridegroom...."
John 3:29a (Capitals are the author's.)

"Let us be glad and rejoice, and give honor to Him: for the marriage of the Lamb is come, and His wife has made herself ready."
Revelation 19:7

Dear One,

Mankind longs to be free naturally, to do as he pleases. The unawakened, unredeemed man is rebellious, blind in his own efforts to be satisfied and happy. I came to show the only way to true freedom and happiness. Until one knows Me, and My truth for themselves, they are deceived in some measure. Therefore, I said, "You must be born again." I am ever revealing Myself to mankind, but pride, selfishness, and fear often stand in the way of seeing Me. I wish to use your life as a story to engage others in recognizing My reality, truth, and power; My Kingdom come.

"Hear, O heavens, and give ear, O earth: for the LORD has spoken, I have nourished and brought up children, and they have rebelled against Me." Isaiah 1:2

Jesus said, *"Marvel not that I said unto you, you must be born again." John 3:7*

Dear Child,

Your longing for Me and My leading in your life relationships and outcomes has an underlying childlike trust. Be assured, I am holding your right hand and keeping you. Yes, you see the suffering and insecurity of others, but do not be shaken by this. Much must be shaken over the world for there to be a vast awakening to Me, and what cannot be shaken. Keep attentive to the good being accomplished through the suffering and shaking. My trusting children are beacons of light in their security, courage, love, and joyful, generous service.

"Therefore I will shake the heavens, and the earth shall remove out of her place, in the wrath of the LORD of hosts, and in the day of His fierce anger." Isaiah 13:13

Jesus said, "You are the light of the world. A city that is set on an hill cannot be hid." Matthew 5:14

Dear Child,

Yes, many find it hard to believe that I am only love and that I love them personally. Consequently, there is the fighting and greed contaminating earth. All need to know that I created them, and want to provide for them. Mankind is deceived into thinking they must, first of all, provide for themselves, and take what they can without limitations. This thinking is entirely backward of reality where My Kingdom, undergirding everything, is sufficient and willing to provide for all if I and it are only recognized and believed as the loving source of everything.

"From whence comes wars and fightings among you? come they not hence, even of your lusts that war in your members? 2 You lust, and have not: you kill and desire to have, and cannot obtain: you fight and war, yet you have not, because you ask not. 3 You ask, and receive not, because you ask amiss, that you may consume it upon your lusts." James 4:1-3

Jesus said, "But seek you first the Kingdom of God, and His righteousness; and all these things shall be added unto you." Matthew 6:33

Dear Child,

Marriage is My idea; My plan for My purposes. I desire your happiness and satisfaction, as well as the continuation of My creation. Prayerful consideration, and choosing of a mate, assures that inner convictions and qualities will find further development and usefulness in My Kingdom. These inner qualities are often acquired and furthered by belief in Me and My Word. Therefore, I said, "Be equally yoked" in your choices to protect and preserve that which is gained through generations of living on earth: knowledge of Me and My love of truth.

"Be you not unequally yoked together with unbelievers:
for what fellowship has righteousness with unrighteousness?
and what communion has light with darkness?" II Corinthians 6:14

"...ordain elders..... 6 If any be blameless, the husband of one wife,
having faithful children not accused of riot or unruly." Titus 1:5b, 6

Dear Child,

I am with you always, in ways you do not always see. I comfort you when all human comfort is gone. I encourage you and strengthen you when you feel weak, and your efforts seem in vain. Accept your humanity, weaknesses, and limitations as invitations to Me, your all present loving Father. Come then to My arms, weeping for joy that I don't abandon My children whom I created for joyful, close companionship.

Jesus said, "...I am with you always, even unto the end of the world.
Amen." Matthew 28:20

"Blessed be God, even the Father of our Lord Jesus Christ,
the Father of mercies, and the God of all comfort." II Corinthians 1:3

Dear Child,

This is a season, only a season of deeper cleansing by fire, My fire. It seems unpleasant, and that you have deceived yourself about your maturity in Me. Not so, My child, I have more for you to do and be. I can trust your motives when you have been cleansed, and purged and pruned by seeing your utter hopeless, depraved heart without My Spirit's filling. I intend to go deeper still. I want you to depend less and less on your own evaluations, opinions, and explanations based upon your past wounds, searches, self-comfort and vindictiveness. Stay close to Me as a trusting daughter. I have more than you can imagine. Be fully where you are for Me! I keep your fire's fuel available; you keep your heart and enjoy the warmth of My love.

> *"How much more shall the blood of Christ,*
> *who through the eternal Spirit offered Himself without spot to God,*
> *purge your conscience from dead works to serve the living God."*
> *Hebrews 9:14*

> *"For our God is a consuming fire." Hebrew 12:29*

Dear Child,

There is no uncertainty in Me. Look within yourself to enjoy the unchanging security of our close fellowship. You turn your attention to Me, often unconsciously, as your source. I am pleased in this. I can easily direct your thoughts and life because you are willing. I reward you even when you can't see it. I know your desires and delights. I give what is good now. Know that I am ahead of you, preparing your future. I love to surprise and please you with how well I know everything about you. In Me, you are not forgotten, overlooked, nor refused My good. Continue to relish every moment as My child, and trust that the future is in My hands of love. You're My daughter in grace, beloved and held close. Your Father.

Jesus said,
"...*behold, the kingdom of God is within you.*"
Luke 17:21

Jesus said, "*Daughter, be of good comfort:
your faith has made you whole; go in peace.*"
Luke 8:48

My Child,

Refuse every thought of fear which tries to run rampant across the world. I am Lord of all. I train My children to rebuke the works of darkness. Sadly, the enemy must be exposed in all his wickedness and consequences of sin. I am ever-present; even able to redeem if I am recognized as the source of all good, and Creator of the universe. Many will now have their eyes opened to My truth and love because of the fear they experience without My hope. Man has caused his troubles and vast unexpected consequences by his foolish thinking and rejection of Me. But, be of good cheer, My little one, I cover you, as a good Father always protects.

"*And Jesus rebuked the devil; and he departed out of him....*"
Matthew 17:18a

"*He shall cover you with His feathers,
and under His wings shall you trust:
His truth shall be your shield and buckler.*"
Psalm 91:4

Summer

Dear Child,

I am your day planner, as you ask. I am always bringing situations and revelations before you for testing, teaching, and tasting Me. No day or moment is wasted in My Kingdom. There are no, uninteresting, purposeless days. There is no need to feel lonely nor despair. I am near and on call, ready to speak, comfort, and show you wondrous things. My Spirit understands you and your true needs. He operates in reality, with delight to do My will, leading, teaching, helping you. See Him as your dearest Friend.

Jesus said, *"And I will pray the Father, and He shall give you another Comforter, that He may abide with you forever." John 14:16*

Jesus said, *"Howbeit when He, the Spirit of truth, is come, He will guide you into all truth: for He shall not speak of Himself; but whatsoever He shall hear, that shall He speak: and He will show you things to come. He shall glorify Me: for He shall receive of Mine, and show it unto you." John 16:13-14*

Dear Child,

Yes, My angels, My messengers, do look after My work on earth. They respond to My directions to guide, help, rescue, and speak. More so, they protect and do justly at times of need. I hear the calls, cries, and petitions of My children and see to the appropriate response. I, Myself, appear at times to confirm My reality and deeply impress where needed. These are days of worldwide unrest and need. My angels are indeed laboring, warning, protecting, and maintaining for Me. Trust you are not alone on earth.

"And, lo, the angel of the Lord came upon them, and the glory of the Lord shone round about them: and they were sore afraid. And the angel said unto them, Fear not: for, behold, I bring you good tidings of great joy, which shall be to all people. For unto you is born this day in the city of David a Savior, which is Christ the Lord." Luke 2:9-11

"And there appeared an angel unto Him from heaven, strengthening Him." Luke 22:43

My Dear Child,

Do not be surprised or troubled by distractions and long suffering that are part of your life. Be blessed that I have given you My Spirit's fruits of patience, love, joy, and yes, long-suffering. Be generous, knowing I bring good out of your interrelationships, no matter how trying, inconvenient or unprofitable they may seem. People grow and flourish because of My Spirit wherever they are attracted to it, as plants do likewise in the sunshine.

"But the fruit of the Spirit is love, joy, peace, longsuffering, gentleness, goodness, faith, meekness, temperance: against such there is no law."
Galatians 5:22-23

"And we know that all things work together for good to them that love God, to them who are the called according to His purpose."
Romans 8:28

Dear Child,

You can consistently find the profoundly satisfying love you want only in Me. You know this to be true, but in human weakness, you often wish for it in people. I came as that human being, for I felt the longing of humanity. Allow Me to comfort your disappointed heart in My way. I reveal My love in unlimited ways, often unexpectedly. Be of good cheer; look up to Me. I will not disappoint My beloved children because I am just and will reward you. I will meet you in the secret place. Love never fails. Take heart.

"Oh that men would praise the Lord for His goodness, and for His wonderful works to the children of men! For He satisfies the longing soul, and fills the hungry soul with goodness." *Psalm 107:8-9*

"He that dwells in the secret place of the most High shall abide under the shadow of the Almighty." *Psalm 91:1*

My Child,

When I look at the earth, your world, I do not see separations of ethnic lands. I see the whole globe and the varied children I have created for My pleasure. I see the ages long story of My children recovering from their separation from Me. I see the many turning to the One Son I have sent to save and help and lead them back to their Father. I gave My children the gift of intellect, speech, and writing to further aid their coming to know Me and follow Me. I gave you the clean, simple way home to Me.

"For the Lord takes pleasure in His people: He will beautify the meek with salvation." Psalm 149:4

"For God sent not His Son into the world to condemn the world; but that the world through Him might be saved." John 3:17

Dear Child,

Am I not the perfect example of steadfastness, consistency, and security? Am I not the One who holds the earth in balance as it turns? Surely, this is evidence of My reality. Likewise, My laws and principles are ever constant, unchanging, and bringing security. In My overseeing, I have left nothing to chance. I have provided all that is needed for life and Godliness. Your role is to see, hear, understand, and obey. From this will come all the joy, pleasure, peace, fruitfulness, and security you need and long for. This is termed salvation.

"Of old have you laid the foundation of the earth: and the heavens are the work of Your hands." Psalm 102:25

"According as His divine power has given unto us all things that pertain unto life and Godliness, through the knowledge of Him that has called us to glory and virtue." II Peter 1:3

Dear Child,

Yes, I speak yet today. I gave the gift of prophesy to My children so they can hear My voice in their time. I have much to say to keep My will freshly before your eyes. I always reinforce My Word with action for those who love My Law. I father My entire church, over all the earth with My words of direction, protection, correction, comfort, and edification. I speak through those of My children who are appointed to lead and through anyone seeking Me and My will. I confirm My truth to whosoever will hear and obey.

"Great peace have they which love your Law: and nothing shall offend them." Psalm 119:165

"But he that prophesies speaks unto men to edification, and exhortation, and comfort." I Corinthians 14:3

My Child,

Each must find and learn to trust Me in their way and time. Instead of lamenting where others might be and lacking in growth, cheerfully use the wisdom and gifts I have given you to disciple those I bring to you. I am God. I am so vast in My creative plan that you cannot grasp what and how I fulfill it in the smallest detail. Do your part with good cheer and even delight. Do not trouble yourself with what seems to be amiss and tragic in the world.

Jesus said, ... "If you continue in My Word, then you are My disciples indeed." John 8:31

"For My thoughts are not your thoughts, neither are your ways My ways, says the Lord. For as the heavens are higher than the earth, so are My ways higher than your ways, and My thoughts than your thoughts." Isaiah 55:8-9

Dear One,

You are discovering the gold of seasons, lived through with Me as a close Companion. The mystery of how I work by My Spirit is more and more revealed to you, as a child discovers everything fresh to it's senses. Sometimes it seems you have, in wonder, missed so much that is now clearly before you. As a good Father, I know My children well, and I know the right time for all growth, protection and rewards. Because you trust Me, I can bless you more and more with Myself and My secrets.

Jesus said, "You are My friends, if you do whatsoever I command you." John 15:14

Jesus said, "Truly I say unto you, Whosoever shall not receive the Kingdom of God as a little child shall in no wise enter therein." Luke 18:17

Dear Child,

How you choose to order your days and your time is up to you. When you come to Me first, it sets the receptive tone for your day. As I bring thoughts, considerations, and situations to your mind, the correct order, priority, and responses become in line with Mine. As friend-to-friend, we come into agreement. You enjoy your place as My child. Your reliance on Me becomes secure, and we co-labor in your life for My purposes and will. Thus this removes burdens, worry and fear from you. You develop gratitude, joy, and a genuine living relationship with Me, constant fellowship.

"My voice shall You hear in the morning, O Lord; in the morning will I direct my prayer unto You, and will look up." Psalm 5:3

"Order my steps in Your Word; and let not any iniquity have dominion over me." Psalm 119:133

Dear Child,

With all My blessings comes the responsibility to use them well; to steward My gifts My way at the right time. This is life long learning for those who desire to mature and know Me. Some will not wait on Me and grasp My blessings for selfish motives too soon. They only acquire the shell of their true desires, and often much sorrow. In this way, usually, My children choose to learn life's lessons the hard way. I am a Father who teaches, trains, and chastens and desires My children to follow My good way. My path brings real fulfillment, completeness, joy, righteousness. and peace.

"The blessing of the Lord, it makes rich, and He adds no sorrow with it." Proverbs 10:22

"My son, despise not the chastening of the Lord; neither be weary of His correction: For whom the Lord loves He corrects; even as a Father the son in whom He delights." Proverbs 3:11-12

Dear Child,

The peace I give is truly beyond your comprehension. When your heart and will follow after Mine, you easily see My hands working My glorious outcomes and growth all around you. This is My Fatherly, original intention for My children. To accomplish this communion, I created the long, ancient story you read in your Bible. I always wait for My children to find Me and My way. Around the world, I make Myself known in many ways, including through My creation. I desire all to know and be saved, finding My peace.

"The works of His hands are verity and judgment; all His commandments are sure." Psalm 111:7

"Be careful for nothing; but in everything by prayer and supplication with thanksgiving let your requests be made known unto God. And the peace of God, which passes all understanding, shall keep your hearts and minds through Christ Jesus." Philippians 4:6-7

Dear Child,

Trust that what you hear from Me is true. So many other voices would want to lure you away, to complicate and distract your attentiveness to Me and My voice. My children know My voice. They are familiar with My tone and quality. I always speak with gentleness, clarity, firmness, and overseeing wise love. Enjoy the security and peace of close communication with Me. I keep your life on the narrow path of simplicity, life-giving thoughts, gracious generosity, and clear purpose. I am the purest of love.

Jesus said, "My sheep hear My voice, and I know them, and they follow Me." John 10:27

Jesus said, "Enter you in at the straight gate: for wide is the gate, and broad is the way, that leads to destruction, and many there be that go in there: Because straight is the gate, and narrow is the way, which leads unto life; and few there be that find it." Matthew 7:13-14

Dear Child,

Do I not prove Myself as the constant, unchanging One in all the fluctuations of life on earth? As you look at your history, can you not see that My Way, My Laws, and My Word are ever true and at work, no matter what man chooses to do? What sorrow, loss, tragedy, and horror would be avoided if mankind would believe Me and honor My Word with obedience. You share My grief at the blindness of mankind to My clear Truth. Go, and do your small part to make Me known, loved, honored, and obeyed.

"Make me to understand the way of Your precepts: so shall I talk of your wondrous works." Psalm 119:27

"Surely he has borne our griefs, and carried our sorrows: yet we did esteem him stricken, smitten of God, and afflicted." Isaiah 53:4

Dear Child,

I am well pleased when you arise and think on Me first; when you look to Me for the new day's plan. I am most pleased when you choose to humble yourself under My hand and obey what you know of Me. You will continually see new glimpses of My hand at work all around you. You will see My Kingdom, which lies behind all that is visible. It will be as hidden treasures reserved only for the humble, lowly ones who seek Me first. You will rejoice as My beloved children for, I am a true Father.

"Humble yourselves therefore under the mighty hand of God, that He may exalt you in due time." I Peter 5:6

"For the invisible things of Him from the creation of the world are clearly seen, being understood by the things that are made, even His eternal power and Godhead; so that they are without excuse." Romans 1:20

Dear Child,

I alone am perfect, perfect in all My ways. I do not condemn you for your imperfections and lapses into sorrow. Take My hand and rise from your self-criticisms. I graciously overlook your weaknesses, and I give you hope to overcome them by My strength. I will purge the sinful thought patterns ingrained from your past as My new mind takes root in you. This is a work of acknowledgment and repentance by you and a work of faith coming by hearing My Word and Me.

"There is therefore now no condemnation to them that which in Christ Jesus, who walk not after the flesh, but after the Spirit." Romans 8:1

"And be not conformed to this world: but be transformed by the renewing of your mind, that you may prove what is that good, acceptable, and perfect, will of God." Romans 12:2

Dear Child,

Yes, I would have you remember the many who suffer in prison for My name's sake in the world. I hear their cries and reply in My voice of strength, comfort, and understanding. Those who are blinded by complacent faith, miss My purpose for lost, darkened humanity. I am ever-enlarging my children's world view and hearts to reach those who do not yet know Me. Out of overflowing love, I ask My children to go to the aid and rescue of humanity, as I direct and send. They are written on My hands.

"Blessed be God, even the Father of our Lord Jesus Christ, the Father of mercies, and the God of all comfort; Who comforts us in all our tribulation, that we may be able to comfort them which are in any trouble, by the comfort wherewith we ourselves are comforted of God." II Corinthians 1:3-4

"Behold, I have graven you upon the palms of My hands; your walls are continually before Me." Isaiah 49:16

Dear Child,

Yes, there is an answer to "why hardships?" When I say, "Take up your cross and follow Me," I am showing the way to a life of gladness and gratitude in whatever place you might find yourself. It may be you need to learn: to put other's needs first, to persevere to accomplish a goal, to lay aside selfishness, selfindulgence or excesses. My agape love covers sin of every kind. In every case, as you turn to me for help, I give the wisdom and strength to do what's right, even a way out if necessary. I endured hardness for you. I invite you to the high way of endurance for Me. I am with you in comfort and fellowship Divine.

"There has no temptation taken you but such as is common to man: but God is faithful, who will not suffer you to be tempted above what you are able; but will with the temptation also make a way to escape, that you may be able to bear it." I Corinthians 10:13

"You therefore endure hardness, as a good soldier of Jesus Christ." II Timothy 2:3

Dear Child,

Yes, love is a very confused, often misused word in the world. All must know they're loved. All need to belong. I put this need within each one from before birth. Sadly, even in the womb, many experience rejection. A new perspective on love is needed. I do not abandon the world I created. My ever-flowing, constant, true love is evident in the very air I give to breathe and all the sun and unseen blessings and care that maintains all life on earth. I am love. I desire you to live a life of love returned to Me, to yourself and others- real, grateful, multiplying agape love.

"And we have known and believed the love that God has to us. God is love; and he that dwells in love dwells in God, and God in him." I John 4:16

Jesus said, "You shall love the Lord your God with all your heart, and with all your soul, and with all your strength, and with all your mind; and your neighbor as yourself." Luke 10:27

Dear Child,

I said, "What does it profit a man to gain the whole world and lose his soul?" Many are blinded by their affairs and successes in the world. They make provision for securing themselves in this life but are deceived by the futility of riches. I alone am the source of true security and the entrance to life eternal. I offer the true riches of righteousness, peace, and joy in My Holy Spirit. Do not give any consideration to the many ways mankind chooses to worship mammon. You have chosen Me, your loving Father, the source of every good thing for you.

Jesus said, "For whosoever will save his life shall lose it: and whosoever will lose his life for My sake shall find it. For what is a man profited, if he shall gain the whole world, and lose his own soul..." Matthew 16:25-26

"For the Kingdom of God is not meat and drink, but righteousness, and peace, and joy in the Holy Spirit." Romans 14:17

Yes, My Child,

Remember, "godliness with contentment is great gain." Only I can judge what is truly just and right. Choose lowliness and meekness. Put aside all comparisons, envy and judgment. It is I who give the desires of the heart in My perfect time to those whose treasure is in Me. Many a saint has foregone life's pleasures and riches for a life of peace and closeness with Me. Recognize what is most valuable in your life, all gifts from Me. You have access to all as My child in My Kingdom today and eternally.

Jesus said, "Blessed are the meek: for they shall inherit the earth."
Matthew 5:5

"For we dare not make ourselves of the number, or compare ourselves with some that commend themselves; but they measuring themselves by themselves, and comparing themselves among themselves, are not wise."
II Corinthians 10:12

Dear Child,

Man has pushed and rejected Me from many places where I once held sway. He has replaced My wisdom and laws with his easy, convenient, pleasure, and greed seeking ones. Therefore, I must allow the vast reaping of what he has sown. Most are blind sheep, following after the "current trends." This grieves Me, as I know the consequences they are choosing. As always, I have a faithful remnant who know Me and understand the times. They speak, write, and pronounce warning truth. Take courage and be one who shows the way out and into My Kingdom.

"Be not deceived: God is not mocked: for whatsoever a man sows, that shall he also reap." Galatians 6:7

"And Jesus, when He came out, saw much people, and was moved with compassion toward them, because they were as sheep not having a shepherd: and He began to teach them many things." Mark 6:34

Yes, My Child,

Much wisdom from Me increases sorrow for the world. Much knowledge can lead to Me and My wisdom. Often, much knowledge can puff one up and cause them to resist knowing Me. As always, it is a choice. It is My mind that influences all thought for good. I would have you walk with a fine delicate balance of wisdom with joy and thanksgiving. Thereby, you are most useful to others. I walk with you, adding daily to both your understanding, wisdom, and ultimate joyful peace. Surrender all to Me and be fully in the world and fully in My Kingdom.

"For in much wisdom is much grief: and he that increases knowledge increases sorrow." Ecclesiastes 1:18

"For Godly sorrow works repentance to salvation not to be repented of: but the sorrow of the world works death." II Corinthians 7:10

Dear Child,

Yes, there are My "bridge people." These people watch and wait for the opportunity to draw the lost, broke, and searching, and walk them to Me and My way. These "bridge people" are secure in My life and Kingdom. They recognize the needs and situations of this world and experience My heart. They have lost their interest in the honors, riches, and pleasures of the world that tries to lure them away from holiness. Their satisfaction, joy and fulfillment lie in seeing others set free to know and enjoy Me with lasting peace, pleasure, and abundant life.

"But watch you in all things, endure afflictions, do the work of an evangelist, make full proof of your ministry." II Timothy 4:5

"For He satisfies the longing soul, and fills the hungry soul with goodness." Psalm 107:9

Dear Child,

I am showing you it is the eleventh hour, the last hour before My return. Most do not recognize the signs of the last days, even though they are clearly before their eyes. I show My prophetic, clear-sighted people what I am doing and what will be in the days ahead. These events and calamities result from seeds of sinful disobedience, selfishness, greed, and excess. I continually speak, warn, and forgive, but man has denied My Word and Me. Do not be troubled nor fearful, as all this must come to pass. Be one who reveals My truth and warns. I still love mankind and desire that none should be lost. Weep with Me for the lost, blind, deaf, confused, and broken.

"Little children, it is the last time: and as you have heard that anti-christ shall come, even now are there many anti-christs; whereby we know that it is the last time." I John 2:18

Jesus said, "Blessed are you that hunger now: for you shall be filled. Blessed are you that weep now: for you shall laugh." Luke 6:21

Dear Child,

Be one who heralds My return to earth. Yes, you will be deemed foolish and naive. Appear foolish for Me. I will use you to speak of My reality as you go about your daily life in many places. As it was when I walked on earth, many cannot and will not recognize Me and follow Me. This is a grievous error. So, I send My followers to the sinning, blinded prisoners, the ones rich in the world's goods, to warn of the strong winds coming and the need of Me as an anchor and refuge. So, go to them without fear or intimidation.

"Knowing this first, that there shall come in the last days scoffers, walking after their own lusts, and saying 'Where is the promise of His coming...' II Peter 3:3-4

"Which hope we have as an anchor of the soul, both sure and steadfast, and which enters into that within the veil." Hebrews 6:19

Dear Child,

I say "little children" because this is your true identity in Me. In the face of My greatness as your Creator Father, the One who made the Universe and beyond, you are little, small. And by embracing your very smallness, you become free of much that would try to entangle you in sinful thoughts and behavior. Meekness, lowliness of mind, gentleness are a part of experiencing your smallness. You must choose your place in My Kingdom to find the rich security of belonging to Me for now and eternity, My sons and daughters.

Jesus said, "Truly I say unto you, Except you be converted, and become as little children, you shall not enter into the Kingdom of heaven." Matthew 18:3

Jesus said, "Take My yoke upon you, and learn of Me; for I am meek and lowly in heart: and you shall find rest unto your souls. For My yoke is easy, and My burden is light." Matthew 11:29-30

Dear Child,

Your weaknesses and inabilities are the common conditions of mankind. Often, you try to hide them or retreat from times of exposure. For Me, however, these are times where I want to meet you and reveal My power and loving purposes. When you recognize your honest condition and begin to look to Me for help, you are on the path to growth and glory. Humility, and taking your place as My child, are the keys to unlock My riches and bring heaven's glory to earth. Face Me, with nothing to hide, and experience My all-sufficiency and peace.

"Therefore I will look unto the Lord; I will wait for the God of my salvation: my God will hear me." Micah 7:7

"Not that we are sufficient of ourselves to think anything as of ourselves; but our sufficiency is of God." II Corinthians 3:5

Yes, My Child,

I often use you to initiate communication with others. It requires My courage and anointing to ask, confront, or correct. My motive is love to heal and reveal the truth. Learn to obey Me in this, and stand strong against any opposing forces. I use My servants to work in My human gardens on earth: planting, weeding, tilling, pruning, harvesting. This is work, not always pleasant, but needed and well rewarded, in time. Do not become discouraged, nor weary. I give seasons and times to rest and be refreshed. Receive my good balance and be strengthened.

"Now he that plants, and he that waters are one: and every man shall receive his own reward according to his own labor." I Corinthians 3:8

"And let us not be weary in well doing: for in due season we shall reap, if we faint not." Galatians 6:9

Dear Child,

When I ask you to teach others, I intend for you to simply and clearly explain what I live in you. You can only give what you've received; that I have established in you. Have no concern for all you do not know. This learning stretches endlessly before you. I need real-life teachers who love My sheep today. As you nurture others, I am silently growing fruit in you that you may be more and more productive in My Kingdom. Don't draw back because of what you may seem to lack. Take courage to draw all from the Vine continually, and trust My perfect teacher, My Holy Spirit.

Jesus said, "…Feed My sheep." John 21:16

Jesus said, "I am the Vine, you are the branches: He that abides in Me, and I in him, the same brings forth much fruit: for without Me you can do nothing." John 15:5

Dear Child,

Surrender to My Spirit is not defeat. I always know and desire what is best for you, bringing the best eventual outcome. As your good Shepherd, I lead to the best food and safety. Wrong and subtle influences abound in the earth world. I oversee protectively to avoid loss and harm to you. It pleases Me when you seek My daily, hourly guidance. This brings you the security, peace, and joy of My desires fulfilled.

Jesus said, "I am the good Shepherd, and know My sheep, and am known of mine." John 10:14

Jesus said, "...And lead us not into temptation; but deliver us from evil." Luke 11:4

Dear Child,

Yes, I am your good, faithful Shepherd. Have I not led you to green, fresh pastures? Here, you can rub against fellow flock members and be led by My true, unfailing, ever fresh Word. I want to shepherd the shepherds of My people if they are willing and courageous. These are the days of confusion and weakness in My flock. I will divide the sheep from the goats in My timing. It's My desire for good shepherds to speak and not waver on My Word at whatever the cost. My sheep must be fed.

"Not forsaking the assembling of ourselves together, as the manner of some is; but exhorting one another: and so much the more, as you see the day approaching." Hebrews 10:25

Jesus said, "And before Him shall be gathered all nations; and He shall separate them one from another, as a Shepherd divides His sheep from the goats." Matthew 25:32

Dear Child,

I invite you to come to Me with your weariness and your earthly concerns. I know your limitations and the seeming demands you feel incapable of bearing. You want to be adequate for all the duties you see are yours. Let Me carry your burdens and lead, one by one, to fulfillment and release. Continue to value every life and person as My gift. Be glad for life on earth. See My assignments as belonging to Me and the outcomes as in My hand. I never give more than you can bear, and I am not pressing you. Do not press yourself.

Jesus said, "Come unto Me, all you that labor and are heavy laden, and I will give you rest." Matthew 11:28

"There has no temptation taken you but such as is common to man: but God is faithful, who will not suffer you to be tempted above what you are able; but will with the temptation also make a way to escape, that you may be able to bear it." I Corinthians 10:13

Dear Child,

I have such a reserve of gifts awaiting you. Your enemy tries to deceive you into poverty, thinking and imagining loss and the need to hoard up. I, your magnanimous, past your imagination, Father, have only thoughts and plans to bless you, to provide lavishly and consistently all that you need, and to fulfill your heart's desires too. I do this in ways to surprise you, delight you, and reveal My smile upon you. Look to My face. I know you, and you can fully trust me to always be with you. I cast away all doubts and fears by My unfathomable love.

"Be not you therefore like unto them: for your Father knows what things you have need of, before you ask him." Matthew 6:8

"There is no fear in love; but perfect love casts out fear...." I John 4:18

Dear Child,

Yes, My Word is a lamp to your path. My light shines on every need and question. It gives unchanging truth that cannot fail. More precious than gold could ever be is My wisdom. You are enriched as you look deep into My Word and apply it to your everyday life. This keeps you close to Me and what is real. Much in the world would deceive you and want to draw you away from My light. Keep your lamp bright, clean, filled with the oil of My Spirit. Shed My light across the world.

"How much better is it to get wisdom than gold! and to get understanding rather to be chosen than silver!" Proverbs 16:16

Jesus said, "But the wise took oil in their vessels with their lamps." Matthew 25:4

Dear Child,

You desire to grow in Me. Therefore, I require truth in your inner life, your motives. When I uncover your selfishness, pride, and mistrust of others and their motives, it's for your growth in truth. I do not condemn you, My child, but ask you to be ever mindful of the log in your eye. Hold to My best vision for each person and relationship, even the costly, unequal ones. I want your fruit to be well, strong, and steadfast. All is well in My love and acceptance of you.

Jesus said, "And why do you behold the mote that is in your brother's eye, but do not consider the beam that is in your eye?" Matthew 7:3

Jesus said, "You have not chosen Me, but I have chosen you, and ordained you, that you should go and bring forth fruit, and that your fruit should remain: that whatsoever you shall ask of the Father in My name, He may give it you. These things I command you, that you love one another." John 15:16-17

Dear Child,

Have I not kept you through rough waters; when you couldn't see through to the storm's end? I hold My beloved children who believe Me and love Me first. I am the consistent, steady anchor for your soul, unchanging in your rapidly changing world. I hold all in perfect balance. I am training My children in My balance: functioning joyfully in the world but sustaining themselves in My eternal Kingdom. Rejoice in thankfulness for My perfect balance.

"Do you know the balancings of the clouds, the wondrous works of Him which is perfect in knowledge?" Job 37:16

"From the end of the earth will I cry unto You, when my heart is overwhelmed: lead me to the rock that is higher than I. For You have been a shelter for me, and a strong tower from the enemy." Psalm 61:2-3

Dear Child,

Put aside your concerns for the future, and an inability to cope with life's demands. Stay within the pleasant boundaries I have laid out for your life. In My Kingdom, less haste and activity can accomplish more. My Spirit only leads in what is truly essential. Many are burdened by excesses of every kind. As always, My burden is easy, enabling you to walk lightly and orderly with Me.

"The Lord is the portion of My inheritance and of my cup: you maintain my lot. The lines are fallen unto me in pleasant places; yes, I have a goodly heritage." Psalm 16:5-6

"Happy is the man that finds wisdom, and the man that gets understanding. Her ways are ways of pleasantness, and all her paths are peace." Proverbs 3:13, 17

Dear Child,

Have you noticed a new calm, strength in your inner self that I am giving you? This will grow, and a peaceful confidence will be more evident to others. I work in slow, steady ways that often suddenly become evident. I want you to be less concerned with how you appear to others and more interested in My touch and impression on others; taking a deeper, genuine interest in their eternal destiny. So, enjoy the growth.

*"But grow in grace, and in the knowledge of
our Lord and Savior Jesus Christ.
To Him be glory both now and for ever. Amen."* II Peter 3:18

*"And they brought young children to Him, that He should
touch them..."* Mark 10:13

Dear Child,

I am pleased that your heart longs for My righteousness and justice, especially in this land. I know and hear the pleas coming to My throne. In My time and way, these shall be granted, though not as you may expect. There's much to be repented of and learned. I am resetting the boundaries for My children. What has been broken down must be rebuilt. Always, I am merciful, yet perfectly just. Trust Me and be at peace.

*"And there is hope in your end, says the Lord, that your children shall
come again to their own border."* Jeremiah 31:17

*"Who is a God like unto You, that pardons iniquity, and passes by the
transgression of the remnant of His heritage? He does not retain His
anger forever, because He delights in mercy."* Micah 7:18

Dear Child,

Have I not made you rich in all that is real and beautiful? Yes, I am the overflowing, generous Father who delights in caring for and surprising His children. And know, I am consistent, unchanging, and be assured I am not finished with restoration in your life. Take My security and be at rest in all I have ahead for you. No man, nor circumstance can take or alter My plan to reward and complete you. Your heart's desire is settled in My generous plan.

"He has made everything beautiful in His time: also He has set the world in their heart, so that no man can find out the work that God makes from the beginning to the end." Ecclesiastes 3:11

"And they that shall be of you shall build the old waste places: you shall raise up the foundations of many generations; and you shall be called, The repairer of the breach, the restorer of paths to dwell in." Isaiah 58:12

Dear Child,

I said, come all who are weary and heavy-laden because I knew you would become so. In no other place can you find the sustaining release, comfort, and strength to go on. My supply has no limits. Depend on Me, moment by moment, and draw what you need. Needy, weak, humble, and asking saves the day! It gives Me joy when you press close to Me for the real, lasting things you need and want. I give them freely.

"But my God shall supply all your need according to His riches in glory by Christ Jesus." Philippians 4:19

"...God resists the proud, and gives grace to the humble. Humble yourselves therefore under the mighty hand of God, that He may exalt you in due time." I Peter 5-6

Dear Child,

Let all anxiety go, my child. My affirmation is enough. I see and understand all. Take no responsibility for the attitudes and evaluations of others. This is My work to care for. Some changes require much time and revelations of My Spirit. Always, one must yield to Me and what I say for true transformation to occur. Receive My love and patience for all, and go your way in peace and joy, beloved and free.

"There is no fear in love; but perfect love casts out fear..." I John 4:18

"Great is our Lord, and of great power: His understanding is infinite." Psalm 147:5

Dear Child,

As you grow deeper in Me, you're beginning to see truths that many are blind to. You recognize the suffering that all must encounter in some way. I allow this for the needed growth towards Me in every life. Your present culture would like to prevent, ignore, and deny the human condition of suffering. Nevertheless, from birth until death, there is some human suffering. It seems a mystery, but all have a purpose. Continually, I offer My joy and peace to those who bear their crosses and yoke with me.

"The Lord opens the eyes of the blind: the Lord raises them that are bowed down: the Lord loves the righteous." Psalm 146:8

Jesus said, "If any man will come after Me, let him deny himself, and take up his cross daily, and follow Me." Luke 9:23

Dear Child,

Have I not supplied every need and more? It's My joy to see My children growing in appreciation of My ways, and gratitude for My abundance. I have much more for you, planned in My goodness and wisdom. You cannot see all the results and effects of your obedience and joy in Me. Love grows and multiplies through your life in its many forms. It has great power and also rewards. Allow Me to command and distribute rewards according to My wisdom. I know your heart's longings, but I desire first your contentment with Me, your Father God.

"...there is a reward for the righteous..." Psalm 58:11

Jesus said, "But seek you first the Kingdom of God, and His righteousness; and all these things shall be added unto you." Matthew 6:33

Dear Child,

I would have My people rally around My banner of love, rather than that of any group or nation. I grieve for the blind adherence to anything that separates, divides, destroys, or stigmatizes My people. My Spirit is poured out on the world to open eyes to the one new man in universal love. I would love that all could see and agree with Me and what I say. One day, I will end all wars, famine, hate between peoples, and all greed and selfishness. Agree with Me today that this time is coming, and find comfort and peace.

"That you put off concerning the former conversation the old man, which is corrupt to the deceitful lusts; and be renewed in the spirit of your mind; and that you put on the new man, which after God is created in righteousness and true holiness." Ephesians 4:22-24

"He brought me to the banqueting house, and His banner over me was love." Song of Solomon 2:4

Dear Child,

I speak to you of sacrificial love. Love that acts out of My great love, not selfishly motivated nor prideful. This is the love of a true parent whose only desire is to see their children free to thrive and prosper. This love is costly and means something must be surrendered for the well being of others. Often, it's misunderstood as weakness or foolishness by those who refuse to feel hurt for others. However, I know and reward this generous love wherever it may be found. Love changes all for the better. I am love.

"And now abides faith, hope, charity, these three; but the greatest of these is charity." I Corinthians 13:13

Jesus said, "Greater love has no man than this, that a man lay down his life for his friends." John 15:13

My Dear Child,

Yes, continue faithfully on the pathway I am and have been leading you. One of quiet, excellent service and care for those needing comfort and healing. Many are the sorrows, hurts, and losses of your world, but I am the oil of restoration and gladness. I call upon you, and My ready servant friends to give out generously and fully; to minister from My great, endless storehouse. Take time, as I lead, to draw away, rest, and be renewed for the rich life I have prepared for you. Receive each new day joyfully, expecting Me to hold your hand. You shall not fail.

"But the path of the just is as the shining light, that shines more and more unto the perfect day." Proverbs 4:18

"You have loved righteousness and hated iniquity; therefore God, even your God, has anointed you with the oil of gladness above your fellows." Hebrews 1:9

Dear Child,

Yes, marriage is a place to work out your greater salvation and your shared transformation. I desire truth in the inward parts; clear, extreme, continuous honesty before Me and each other. Thereby, I can cleanse the past from the generations of blindness, uncleanness, selfishness, and hurts of pridefulness. Much has been cleansed, but not all. Be assured; I'll complete the work I've begun in both. Tear not up at each other. Pour the oil of healing and joy on one another as I have many in need of your hope, example, and testimony. Be My very honest children.

"Behold, You desire truth in the inward parts: and in the hidden part You shall make me to know wisdom." Psalm 51:6

"Being confident of this very thing, that He which has begun a good work in you will perform it until the day of Jesus Christ." Philippians 1:6

Yes, My Child,

I am the great trainer, and I am all present to you in your world. I coach you: I put challenges before you and answer prayers for your success. Each success prepares you for greater strength, self control, and My ultimate fruitfulness. Your soul never reaches finished training, and indeed finds My ongoing discipline a great refiner. Welcome My correction, rebuke, and cleansing. You will come to know Me very well as a loving, all-wise Father who must train His children. Those who refuse My soul training go through life blind, poor, and unhappy. Be a grateful, learning child, and enjoy the very best of life with Me.

"Behold, happy is the man whom God corrects: therefore, do not despise the chastening of the Almighty." Job 5:17

"…he is like a refiner's fire, and like fuller's soap." Malachi 3:2

Dear Child,

Forgive yourself for much weakness and falling back to old lifeless behavior. I do not condemn you; I forgive. I know you are but dust. I see the harsh conditions around you and the sadness that comes upon you for all the pains of earth. I see the little consolation of slow or no change in humanity. All this works to discourage you. Remember Me; I am not discouraged by earth's woes and human weaknesses that seem so hopeless. Remember My open arms to the prodigal son. I embraced and restored him as I do you today. Take comfort now as My beloved, belonging child.

"He has not dealt with us after our sins; nor rewarded us according to our iniquities. For as the heaven is high above the earth, so great is His mercy toward them that fear Him. As far as the east is from the west, so far has He removed our transgressions from us. Like as a Father pities His children, so the Lord pities them that fear Him. For He knows our frame; He remembers that we are dust." Psalm 103:10-14

"...But when he was yet a great way off, his Father saw him, and had compassion, and ran, and fell on his neck, and kissed him." Luke 15:20

Yes, Dear Child,

I am the healer of every hurt, misfortune, and sickness. But, one must call upon the physician, seek His counsel, and act on it. Too often, faith is placed elsewhere and not in Me. Many turn to that which has no merit or goodness to them, persisting in false methods and medicines. My medicine is My original design that needs to be recognized and allowed to function. Also, there is much on earth that contributes to healing, but this is often unrecognized or ignored. To some are given the gifts of healing and helps. These understand Me, My Word, and ways. I lead and direct to My servants of healing.

"…yet in his disease he did not seek the Lord, but went to the physicians." II Chronicles 16:12

"Is any sick among you? Let him call for the elders of the church; and let them pray over him, anointing him with oil in the name of the Lord: and the prayer of faith shall save the sick, and the Lord shall raise him up; and if he has committed sins, he shall be forgiven." James 5:14-15

"…the gifts of healing are given to another by the same Spirit." I Corinthians 12:7-9

Dear Child,

Do not trouble yourself over the adjustments needed by life's external circumstances. My constancy should be your focus; neither concern yourself about being judged or misunderstood by others. Most have no time for nor interest in you or your concerns. Make Me the priority in all these circumstances and rejoice in My calm presence and peace. I have called and supplied you, and this increases in the measure of the needs around you. Serve Me in joy at My sufficiency. Help others to find Me and hope for their lives; encouraged in the chaos. I order the righteous's steps, and My blood assures the final outcome of holiness for whosoever will come to Me.

"...the goodness of God endures continually." Psalm 52:1

"Now the God of peace, that brought again from the dead our Lord Jesus, that great shepherd of the sheep, through the blood of the everlasting covenant, make you perfect in every good work to do His will, working in you that which is well pleasing in His sight, through Jesus Christ; to whom be glory forever and ever. Amen." Hebrews 13:20-21

My Dear Child, waiting upon Me,

I am here with you. I know the wearying of earth's increasing sorrows and confusion. Yet, I said these times must come to usher in My return. Have I not said, there is much sorrow in knowing My wise counsel and Me? For this, I say rejoice and be glad in My gifts. Take the garment of praise for the spirit of heaviness. Remember, you are set apart for My life of praise and communion, not a life of striving after wind. Your desired haven of service has been provided and secured from strife. Notice how rare and rich is your place in My Kingdom. Extend My love, wise counsel, and care to all whose lives you touch. Be calm in the storm.

"To appoint unto them that mourn in Zion, to give them beauty for ashes, the oil of joy for mourning, the garment of praise for the spirit of heaviness; that they might be called trees of righteousness, the planting of the Lord, that He might be glorified." Isaiah 61:3

"For they have sown the wind, and they shall reap the whirlwind..." Hosea 8:7

Fall

Yes, My Child,

Your memories, dreams, hopes, talents, and giftings are often related to those who went before you in life. --even those you do not know, never met, and did not know of your coming in their future family line. I am a God who thinks in generations, preserving and ever creating the new. A grateful heart for your life, those who contribute to it, and your legacy are what make you rich. Enjoy the deep, everlasting riches in Me, your Lord and Father.

"Remember the days of old, consider the years of many generations: ask your father, and he will show you; your elders and they will tell you."
Deuteronomy 32:7

"As you have therefore received Christ Jesus the Lord, so walk you in Him. Rooted and built up in Him, and established in the faith, as you have been taught, abounding therein with thanksgiving." Colossians 2:6-7

Dear Child,

Indeed, I am a shield for My people. In Me, they have My significance, My glory. I lift their heads above the expectations and harassment of the world. They do not need to conform to the beliefs of those who do not believe in Me. In this, they are indeed set apart for My life in them and My purposes. I enlarge their hearts and clear their minds to look upon all with My compassion and wisdom. My Spirit trains them. Day by day, their inner life is enriched by Me, and their place in the world is as a well-watered, living garden."

"But You, O Lord, are a shield for me; my glory, and the lifter of my head." Psalm 3:3

"But know that the Lord has set apart him that is Godly for Himself: the Lord will hear when I call unto Him." Psalm 4:3

Dear Child,

As is often the case, for those who follow Me, I ask them to wait. Because I am at work to place people and circumstances in My order, it may appear that waiting is of no use or importance. Because you live in the realm of time and space, it seems to take longer than you would like for prayer to be answered. Use your waiting time wisely to make inquiries of Me and hear My words of revelation and comforting encouragement. I am always speaking to those who have ears to hear.

"Lead me in your truth, and teach me: for you are the God of my salvation; on you do I wait all the day." Psalm 25:5

Jesus said, "Who has ears to hear, let him hear." Matthew 13:9

Yes, My Child,

Those who truly know Me are a small minority globally, but the number is steadily growing. There are those who long for and await My bodily return to earth, as they know I am coming for My own. No pressure from you can hasten My return. Your place is to rest, calmly living out My Words and making Me known as I direct. I give you more peace, and I desire you to receive it. The pressure you put upon yourself is neither productive nor from Me. Follow My gentle leading beside still water and green pastures.

Jesus said, "And if I go and prepare a place for you, I will come again, and receive you unto Myself; that where I am, there you may be also." John 14:3

Jesus said, "It is not for you to know the times or the seasons, which the Father has put in His own power." Acts 1:7

Dear Child,

I enlarge your heart to care for and desire to nurture others to become whom I created them to be. But, you do not have the power to make this happen. I am the Great Provider. The multitude of gifts I make available is needed for this endeavor. In this, I ask you to work with Me as a gardener works. I am the glory light that causes all life to grow and multiply. I draw you to sit in My glory light and be filled, enlightened, healed, and strengthened. This equips you with faith gifts for every need and challenge. My great mind power, compassion, and generosity are needed for every lasting work to be successful.

Jesus said, "I am the vine, you are the branches: He that abides in Me, and I in him, the same brings forth much fruit: for without Me you can do nothing." John 15:4

Jesus said, "You have not chosen Me, but I have chosen you, and ordained you, that you should go and bring forth fruit, and that your fruit should remain: that whatsoever you shall ask of the Father in My name, He may give it to you." John 15:16

Dear Child,

Those who want to live Godly lives in Jesus will encounter persecution. You know, multitudes are living secret lives with me. I cherish them and strengthen them and protect them. I make Myself known where it is forbidden to know Me. I will have followers from every people group. Rapidly, I am revealing Myself, My Word, and My voice around the world. I want the little children to also come to Me. I am drawn to the lonely, hurt, confused, and lost. It's My desire for all to hear Me and discover My sufficiency for all of life's sorrows.

"Yes, and all that will live godly in Christ Jesus shall suffer persecution." II Timothy 3:12

"And I saw another angel fly in the midst of heaven, having the ever-lasting gospel to preach unto them that dwell on the earth, and to every nation, and kindred, and tongue and people." Revelation 14:6

Dear Child,

Yes, I am with you in the hidden garden of your inner, true life with Me. There, none of earth's troubles can reach you. As I said, you will have tribulations and sorrows on earth, but in Me, you can overcome them. Keep this perspective and place in balance with the mercy, compassion and help to serve others. Isolation and denial are not the healing attitudes for My work on earth. For this, I give courage and all My Spirit's gifts. Each person has a purpose to bring My life in some way or place. Happy are those who find Me, their place, and their purpose. Seek Me first.

"...and their soul shall be as a watered garden; and they shall not sorrow any more at all." Jeremiah 31:12

"Let all those that seek You rejoice and be glad in you: and let such as love Your salvation say continually, Let God be magnified." Psalm 70:4

Dear Child,

When I say cast all your cares on Me, I mean just that. Release them to My hands one by one. Be quiet before Me. Go on like a little child, to the next interesting attraction. Trust I know, care, and heard your concerns. I enjoy hearing about your desires, hopes, and dreams. Your open heart and hands delight Me. I want to give you more gifts and joy than you can imagine. They are poured out continually. The air, clouds, sun, water, and all creation that sustains you and life around you are My limitless gifts. Recognize My love in all it's power and forms.

"Cast your burden upon the Lord, and He shall sustain you: He shall never suffer the righteous to be moved." Psalm 55:22

"Every good gift and every perfect gift is from above, and comes down from the Father of lights, with whom is no variableness, neither shadow of turning." James 1:17

Dear Child,

We both experience great joy and pleasure as we bring forth fruit in season, and I prosper you. I create the seasons with fresh varieties of fruit. In the later seasons of life, I expect an abundance of wisdom, grace, and generosity with the rich deposits I've made in you through years of following Me. Some harvest much in a few years, but long life is My gift to stretch out the pleasure. In the early years of life, children are close to Me, so it should be at the closing years. Be as a little child in the sweetest of seasons. Show how real is My great love.

"And he shall be like a tree planted by the rivers of water, that brings forth his fruit in his season; his leaf also shall not wither; and whatsoever he does shall prosper." Psalm 1:3

"Those that be planted in the house of the Lord shall flourish in the courts of our God. They shall still bring forth fruit in old age; they shall be fat and flourishing." Psalm 92:13-14

Dear Child,

Yes, I speak in every language and without language. I designed you with a system of nerves and an extraordinary brain beyond your comprehension. I am the Great Communicator. I speak to all mankind in some way, as all are created in My pattern. So much is coded into your bodies that you could never know entirely. Sadly, this is often not recognized, cared for, and nurtured to find the fullness I desire. My plan is for mankind to know Me and use their resources to bless others and build My Kingdom. Build with me and enjoy the abundance that reaches eternity.

"And God said, Let us make man in our image, after our likeness..." Genesis 1:26

"And they shall not teach every man his neighbor, and every man his brother, saying, Know the Lord: for all shall know Me, from the least to the greatest." Hebrews 8:11

Dear Child,

You are troubling your self, like Martha, over many small matters. The time you live in presses many to overdo, overthink and overindulge. These are not My thoughts. My Word speaks to you of the basic life matters in simple, clear wisdom. For the hungry, this is satisfaction and direction enough. Train yourself in My ways, and allow My Spirit to counsel you in every part of your life. He will keep you in balanced simplicity, quiet, calm peace, and the eternal pleasures at My right hand.

Jesus said, "Martha, Martha, you are careful and troubled about many things." Luke 10:41

"You will show me the path of life: in Your presence is fullness of joy; at your right hand there are pleasures for evermore." Psalm 16:11

Dear Child,

Yes, there is a fine line between taking Me for granted, and not knowing Me at all. Therefore, I made a relationship with Me available to whomsoever seeks Me. The temple veil was torn to show that I am available to be known in My reality. As you know others by observation and words, you can know and enjoy a relationship with Me by hearing Me and seeing My words confirmed by My ways. Many live empty, confused, and fruitless lives because they do not know Me personally. Be My child who shows that I am real and sent My Son out of great love for them.

"God is faithful, by whom you were called unto the fellowship of His Son Jesus Christ our Lord." I Corinthians 1:9

Jesus said," For God so loved the world, that He gave His only begotten Son, that whosoever believes in Him should not perish, but have everlasting life." John 3:16

Dear Child,

When I say rest to you, I do not necessarily mean more time asleep. I speak of an attitude of centering on My peaceful, non-hurried nature where all is accomplished in My good and perfect time. So much joy is lost when you rush from job to job and place to place. My intention is for you to realize and receive the glory and goodness around you in a meaningful, delightful appreciation. I am giving you every good thing, and you cannot forget the Giver in your everyday living.

"Be careful for nothing; but in everything by prayer and supplication with thanksgiving let your requests be made know unto God. And the peace of God, which passes all understanding, shall keep your hearts and minds through Christ Jesus. Philippians 4:6-7

"Let this mind be in you, which was also in Christ Jesus...." Philippians 2:5

Dear Child,

Turn your attention towards Me when a wrong thought tries to enter your mind. Find safety in My mind of only right, just, pure, humble thoughts. Rebuke every one that you know does not fit with My nature and Word. Remain in your inner spirit with me, and do not be drawn into foolishness, evil imaginations, lies, and lack of self-control. I always point to a way out of these situations. This is how you walk in the light, as I am in the light. Humanly, you often fail, but I do not condemn you. I draw you back, and by My Spirit, I teach you aright. Be a good learner, and even teach others to do My will.

"Finally, brethren, whatsoever things are true, whatsoever things are honest, whatsoever things are just, whatsoever things are pure, whatsoever things are lovely, whatsoever things are of good report; if there be any virtue, and if there be any praise, think on these things. Those things, which you have both learned, and received, and heard, and seen in me, do: and the God of peace shall be with you. Philippians 4:8-9

"And the LORD said unto Satan, the LORD rebuke you, O Satan..." Zechariah 3:2

Dear Child,

Please calm yourself to listen. Be a good, quiet listener. Following Me in obedience does not mean pressuring yourself to be good or to perfect yourself. It means keeping your focus on Me. Following Me, you abide under My shadow, safely, gently looking to My leadership. I fully understand the difficulties of life on earth; how you must work to keep up that which is continually changing and demanding your attention. I came to enable you to overcome, day by day, the consequences of sin. I sent you My Spirit to help and comfort. Listen to Him.

"He that dwells in the secret place of the Most High shall abide under the shadow of the Almighty. I will say of the Lord, He is my refuge and my fortress: My God; in Him will I trust." Psalm 91:1-2

Jesus said, "But the Comforter, which is the Holy Spirit, whom the Father will send in My Name, He shall teach you all things, and bring all things to your remembrance, whatsoever I have said unto you." John 14:26

My Child,

Do not attempt to enter into My grief, the grief of My Spirit concerning the earth's condition, and the history of My people. Some things you cannot comprehend at this time. I do not desire this great heaviness of your heart. Your destiny is to interest yourself in the well being and growth of those immediately around you. Yes, you may prayerfully care about world conditions, but you must give Me the burdens I do not intend for you. Better to walk lightly with Me, showing many how to live abundantly and joyfully now in the middle of darkness.

"Surely He has borne our griefs, and carried our sorrows…" Isaiah 53:4

"For, behold, the darkness shall cover the earth, and gross darkness the people: but the Lord shall arise upon you, and His glory shall be seen upon you." Isaiah 60:2

Yes, My Child,

A merry heart brings a continual feast of nourishing faith in My goodness and continuous relationship with Me and others. Living in My presence brings steady security, hope, and joy that can come from no other source. There's no need to seek out remedies for loneliness, rejection, fear and boredom. Man's isolation, independence, and sin sickness stem from an ancient separation from me. I sent My Son Jesus to open the way back to me, the Father of all life, the Divine Mind, and Companion. My will is for you to know and enjoy Him and make Him known.

"…he that is of a merry heart has a continual feast." Proverbs 15:15

Jesus said, *"For the Son of man is come to save that which was lost."* Matthew 18:11

Yes, My Child,

You are serving Me most effectively when it is with glad, cheerful thoughts of thankfulness. Wherever you are, this is noted and often admired and sometimes imitated. This is faith and praise in action. I intend My children to be noticeably distinct and supernatural in their everyday living. For this, I say be wise, as well as gently dependent upon My Spirit's leading. Exercise your mind to keep your thoughts on Me and My Word. Following Me in this way keeps you secure, tender-hearted, and most influential in the work of My Kingdom.

Jesus said, *"Behold, I send you forth as sheep in the midst of wolves: be you therefore wise as serpents, and harmless as doves."* Matthew 10:16

"Serve the Lord with gladness: come before His presence with singing." Psalm 100:2

My Child,
Wear the garment of praise. Avoid too long a look at the darkness in the world, the burden of heaviness. Notice a happy child does not linger long on a serious thought. Soon, they will turn to the next matter of interest and wonder. I am always revealing a new thing as you stay close to Me and think My thoughts. Walk in My light, looking ahead, focused on Me. As the earth continually turns, so I am always making all things new. Even your physical body does not remain fixed. So, rejoice in each new morning of changing life with Me. Be fully, freely alive.

"To appoint unto them that mourn in Zion, to give unto them beauty for ashes, the oil of joy for mourning, the garment of praise for the spirit of heaviness; that they might be called trees of righteousness, the planting of the Lord, that He might be glorified." Isaiah 61:3

"And He that sat upon the throne said, Behold, I make all things new. And He said unto me, Write: for these words are true and faithful." Revelation 21:5

Dear Child,
Keep your focus on now, today with Me. There is courage and steadfastness to meet every need and challenge. Do not allow yourself to be pulled into the rushing thoughts of all that needs to be accomplished and the related worries. Learn how to take hold of these thoughts and be obedient to My thoughts. As with all learning, you begin with practice and repetition. All change and growth form in your mind with your thoughts. Saturate yourself in the truth of My Word and My ever-present help. Go from grace to victory to glory.

"Casting down imaginations, and every high thing that exalts itself against the knowledge of God, and bringing into captivity every thought to the obedience of Christ..." II Corinthians 10:5

"And be not conformed to this world: but be transformed by the renewing of your mind, that you may prove what is that good, and acceptable, and perfect, will of God." Romans 12:2

Dear Child,

There are lessons to be learned right before your eyes. The moving earth creates shadows from the sun that are temporary. The sun, like My love, is unchanging and constant. There is a purpose for the shadows of cooling, quieting, and correcting times. These are needed on earth. Gratefully receive these times as also from My hand. Without them, you may strive to make your life an exhausting run after successes, accumulation, and the approval of man. Therefore, I said, "In everything give thanks" and "...take My peace and rest." Follow Me, and find the perfect balance that brings wholeness and shalom.

"And the work of righteousness shall be peace; and the effect of righteousness quietness and assurance forever." Isaiah 32:17

"Behold, happy is the man whom God corrects: therefore, do not despise the chastening of the Almighty." Job 5:17

Dear Child,

Recognize the wondrous body I have given you, intertwined with your soul of thoughts, emotions, and willpower. Also, I have given you a spirit to relate with My Spirit. Often, this spirit lies dormant, unrecognized by those who are not born again. This is you, indeed, a fearfully created person. I placed such great value on you that I planned in detail the sacrifice of My dear Son to save and redeem you. When you gratefully accept and receive Him as your treasure, your heart follows and settles on Him alone. Thereby, you receive access to My storehouse of every good gift I make available to My children.

"And the very God of peace sanctify you wholly; and I pray God your whole spirit and soul and body be preserved blameless unto the coming of our Lord Jesus Christ." I Thessalonians 5:23

Jesus said, *"Marvel not that I said unto you, You must be born again." John 3:7*

Dear Child,

Just as one exotic bloom can quietly fragrance an entire room, so can a prayerful person lift and cleanse the atmosphere around them. There is pleasure and release in continuous surrender to My will that nothing else can bring. Many look outwardly to lift and cover their needs in many short-lived ways. This is the wide way that leads to death and continued blindness. You can direct them to My narrow path that only leads to abundant eternal life and pleasures. The Kingdom of God is within.

Jesus said, "Enter in at the straight gate: for wide is the gate, and broad is the way, that leads to destruction, and many there be which go in thereat: Because straight is the gate, and narrow is the way, which leads unto life, and few there be that find it." Matthew 7:13-14

Jesus said, "...the Kingdom of God is within you." Luke 17:21

Dear Child,

There are many places you could call when help is needed. As your attention is inwardly, continuously focused on Me, I should be your first call. I am there with all wisdom and knowledge of your situation and condition. I want to bring immediate awareness of what is needed and make it available. Again, I say, remember your place as My child, no matter your earthly age in years. Remember My role as your committed, unchanging, ever-present Father. I am the original Father from whom all fathers receive everything good to give.

"I will call upon the Lord, who is worthy to be praised: so shall I be saved from my enemies." Psalm 18:3

Jesus said, "When you pray, say, Our Father which art in heaven, Hallowed be your Name. Your Kingdom come, Your will be done, as in heaven, so in earth." Luke 11:2

Dear Child,

Surrendering often comes in steps. Naturally, you want to hold onto yourself, your possessions, your life control. However, My Kingdom and power are what you know as supernatural. All you have for now has come from My hands. I know best how to use it.

Furthermore, when you release yourself to Me, I can multiply your small offerings thousands of times over as I did the loaves and fishes. Those who served out the bread and fishes were also satisfied. Let love for Me and others overcome the fear of lack. I always promise sufficiency and My wondrous abundance to those who believe, surrender and obey.

"Now He that ministers seed to the sower both ministers bread for your food, and multiplies your seed sown, and increases the fruits of your righteousness." II Corinthians 9:10

Jesus said," He that finds his life shall lose it, and he that loses his life for My sake shall find it." Matthew 10:39

Dear Child,

I never give you more than you can bear unless I show you a true, often gentle, exit. Keep turning your attention and listening ears to Me in situations of pressure and need. More often, it's the needs, demands, and expectations of others that add heaviness to your life. You may believe or imagine you need to be more or different from who I created you to be. For these reasons, I have said I am a friend, closer than family. You can always lean on Me for true acceptance, wisdom to respond in life, and the strength of character you lack. I am a very present help in all trouble. You are not alone.

"There has no temptation taken you but such as is common to man: but God is faithful, who will not suffer you to be tempted above what you are able; but will with the temptation also make a way to escape, that you may be able to bear it." I Corinthians 10:13

"...there is a Friend that sticks closer than a brother." Proverbs 18:34

My Dear Child,

As you read and meditate on history, notice that many of Abraham's children were entrenched in their religious observances and did not receive Me as their own Messiah. So it is in your time, many will accept a leader who will seem to save them from the world's deep problems, allowing them to continue in comfortable religion. Those who truly know Me will pay the price for continuing to wait upon Me and My return to earth. False saviors will again deceive and lead many astray. But, wait and stay faithful until I come. Do not be deceived in the days ahead.

Jesus said, *"For there shall arise false Christs, and false prophets, and shall show great signs and wonders; insomuch that, if it were possible, they shall deceive the very elect."* Matthew 24:24

Jesus said, *"But he that shall endure unto the end, the same shall be saved."* Matthew 24:13

My Dear Child,

Truly, I am the Great Listener. This is most difficult for you to imagine. I hear all on earth. I especially hear the words and hearts of those who follow Me and those who search and seek Me. Be comforted in knowing My steadfastness; I do not waver. There is some training needed to hear Me consistently and clearly. My sheep learn to know My voice and be glad for it. You grow in wisdom as you reflect on Me as you experience your life on earth. Be one of My most fruitful and useful servants with ready ears.

"With my whole heart have I sought You: O let me not wander from Your commandments." Psalm 119:10

"I have taught you in the way of wisdom; I have led you in right paths." Proverbs 4:11

Dear Child,

Many are lost in unbelief because they do not see nor understand how My Word can be true. For this reason, they choose to be their own god, attempting to control their own lives. Thereby, their ability to receive and give in the world is vastly limited. Their joy, contentment, peace, and meaning in life are uncertain and shifting. I am that Rock on which a secure life is built. Even those who live closest to Me cannot fully understand all that I am and do. There are vast mysteries in the universe that are reserved for eternity and your place in it. Find Me, and know contentment and peace in My embrace and leading; being My child.

"...the Lord is my rock, and my fortress and my deliverer."
II Samuel 22:2

"Your Word is a lamp unto my feet, and a light unto my path."
Psalm 119:105

Dear Child,

Yes, I reward those who diligently seek Me. They shall eventually discover that I am real and true to My Word. Much in life on earth is a poor shadow of what is real in My Kingdom. On earth, rewards are given for accomplishments. These rewards have limits. My rewards are limitless and stretch into eternity; to re-ward means to give again territory. I also give territory to those who overcome themselves by My power. Those who are filled with My powerful Spirit take greater territory for Me and My Kingdom. This is My great reward for humble, courageous obedience and love demonstrated to the world.

"But without faith it is impossible to please Him: for he that comes to God must believe that He is, and that He is a rewarder of them that diligently seek Him." Hebrews 11:6

"And when they had prayed, the place was shaken where they were assembled together; and they were all filled with the Holy Spirit, and they spoke the Word of God with boldness." Acts 4:31

My Dear Child,

When I say do not judge another, I say it for your well-being. You cannot know all the facts concerning another's life. Furthermore, when you judge, you push Me aside and try to take My place. I alone am the all-knowing, everywhere present God. I give you wisdom, knowledge, discernment, and prophecy to understand whatever you face and to make the right responses, but you must remember I am your source. I decide what is best for you to know as you co-labor with Me. Always remember your dependent place as My child led by My Spirit.

"For to one is given by the Spirit the word of wisdom; to another the word of knowledge by the same Spirit; to another faith...; to another the gifts of healing...; to another the working of miracles; to another prophecy; to another discerning of spirits; to another different kinds of tongues; to another the interpretation of tongues." I Corinthians 12:8-10

"For we are laborers together with God: you are God's husbandry, you are God's building." I Corinthians 3:9

Dear Child,

I am making Myself known over all the earth in ways that would have been unthinkable and impossible in past times. Just as I will complete in you the work I have begun, so I will complete the work I have begun in creating the world. For you who have eyes to see and ears to hear, know that I am following My creation plan and the end of all things. Look up, and rejoice that you are a part of My plan of redemption and love in sending My Son to show the way back to Me. These are days of powerful awakening in all the earth. Labor on joyfully and receive My servant's reward.

"Being confident of this very thing, that He who has begun a good work in you will perform it until the day of Jesus Christ." Philippians 1:6

"Wherefore God also has highly exalted Him, and given Him a name which is above every name: And that at the name of Jesus, every knee should bow, of things in heaven, and things in earth, and things under the earth. And that every tongue should confess that Jesus Christ is Lord, to the glory of God the Father." Philippians 2:9-11

Yes, My Child,

You see and consider that it is My nature to give. All that you enjoy and need I have provided. I even meet needs you do not recognize. Your inner drive for belonging, security, and affirmation are there from the beginning of life. You are propelled on to live because of these desires. My purpose is for you to be a seeker and adventurer, growing towards Me and discovering Me. Be a good and gracious giver, hand in hand with Me, bringing others along the narrow, joyful way home to Me.

"Grace and peace be multiplied unto you through the knowledge of God, and of Jesus our Lord. According as His Divine power has given unto us all things that pertain unto life and godliness, through the knowledge of Him that has called us to glory and virtue." II Peter 1:2-3

"But this I say, he which sows sparingly, shall reap also sparingly; and he which sows bountifully shall reap also bountifully. Every man according as he purposes in his heart, so let him give; not grudgingly, or of necessity: for God loves a cheerful giver." II Corinthians 9:6-7

My Dear Child,

Sing, for indeed I am the Savior of the world. I came to the middle of the world, where I planted my people's first home; those selected to reveal Me to the world. Because I chose them, they have endured the greatest suffering and loss, as mankind rejected Me and them. By accepting and loving them and Me, you add to their hope, salvation, and restoration. I restore all losses and make all things new for those who call Me Father. This is indeed a mystery to you but will one day be clear and recognized in eternity.

"...I am the Lord God of Abraham your father, and the God of Isaac: the land whereon you lie, to you I will give it, and to your seed. And your seed shall be as the dust of the earth, and you shall spread abroad to the west, and to the east, and to the north, and to the south: and in your seed shall all the families of the earth be blessed." Genesis 28:13-14

Dear Child,

Trust there is meaning and My purpose in times and situations you do not understand. I have formed you in such a way that your earliest memories and circumstances lay the foundation for your life. Little of this was under your control, but it remains a deep, powerful part of your nature. At learning times of revelation, I bring these memories to your conscience remembrance. This is to assure you I made no mistakes, and I know and love you individually. I am instructing you in the way you should go as you ponder these memories. Truly, My goal is thankfulness as I draw you to Myself, your original Father.

"I will instruct you and teach you in the way which you shall go:
I will guide you with My eye." Psalm 32:8

"Forasmuch as you know that you were not redeemed with corruptible
things, as silver and gold, from your vain conversation received
by tradition from your fathers; But with the precious blood of Christ,
as of a lamb without blemish and without spot." I Peter 1:18-19

Yes, Dear Child,

You do well to hail Me as the Savior of the world. There is no place, no heart I do not wish to enter into and make Myself known. Where I and My Word are honored and believed, there becomes room for man's responsibility to others and a longing for things of the Spirit. What is termed culture is the flow of My love and wisdom out into ordinary people's lives for their good. Against the tempting pull of man's enemy, there is always My greater draw of love, wisdom, peace, and positive creativity. I am always at work, saving, protecting, restoring, and helping mankind in My love.

"Be not overcome of evil, but overcome evil with good." Romans 12:21

"And now abides faith, hope, charity, these three;
but the greatest of these is charity."
I Corinthians 13:13

Dear Child,

Yes, I bring beauty from ashes. But, even ugly, dead ashes have a purpose in My plan. When ashes of failure and broken dreams bring you to true conviction of sin and genuine repentance, I am pleased. Some choose to hide or ignore or defend their weaknesses and sins. They reject, in fear, the possibility of bright beauty and hope. My desire is a clean, humble confession, so I can to bring you to a new, beautiful beginning beyond all that you could ask or think. I am the origin of all that is beautiful, your true Father.

"And they which heard it, being convicted by their own conscience, went out one by one..." John 8:9

"Now unto Him that is able to do exceeding abundantly above all that we ask or think, according to the power that works in us, Unto Him be glory in the church by Christ Jesus throughout all ages, world without end. Amen." Ephesians 3:20-21

Dear Child,

I said I am with you ALWAYS. Believe Me, and do not despair in times of human weakness. Be absolved of guilt, real or imagined. Receive a clean heart and right spirit from Me. There is much in your earthly environment that is unclean, but My Spirit in you can remain untouched by the outer darkness. I lead you to avoid deception, confusion, sin, and filth. I protect you as a Father protects His vulnerable child. Receive My peace and comfort, knowing I do not reject you ever.

"Create in me a clean heart, O God; and renew a right spirit within me. Cast me not away from your Presence; and take not your Holy Spirit from me." Psalm 51:10-11

"When my father and my mother forsake me, then the Lord will take me up." Psalm 27:10

Dear Child,

Inner beauty, balance, and a genuine interest in other's well-being stem from My love and consistent abiding in Me. These endure, as outer circumstances may change. In this way, I create a rich and rewarding life. When such a life is lived, there grows wisdom and a satisfying fulfillment of My purposes, even in an obscure and quiet life. You can see My law of sowing and reaping in effect all around you. Love, My love, never fails to bring a life-giving flow to all it touches.

Jesus said, "Abide in Me, and I in you. As the branch cannot bear fruit of itself, except it abide in the vine; no more can you, except you abide in Me." John 15:4

"...Charity never fails..." I Corinthians 13:8

Dear Child,

Remember, I make all things new. Nothing remains stagnant, although it may appear to be so. Even that which breaks down is a part of becoming something new. Nothing escapes My oversight. I give My children ever new and expanding revelation as we partner together to make things new and better. Growing and maturing into what I have in My mind should be a deep delight and satisfaction to you. Freely release yourself to total fulfillment in Me, showing others how good is all My work and blessing.

"For, behold, I create new heavens and a new earth..." Isaiah 65:17

"...His compassions fail not. They are new every morning: great is Your faithfulness." Lamentations 3:22-23

Dear Child,

Go forward, always forward, letting the past go. Glean the wisdom and grow on to become the complete person in Me. I am ever-renewing and refreshing My children. I carry them through experiences to teach them about Myself and My ways, My laws. Remember, this is your life purpose; to know and relish that knowledge of Me and what is real and eternal. I expect you to keep this in mind as you overcome the sorrows and losses of living the earth's experiences.

"Brethren, I count not myself to have apprehended: but this one thing I do, forgetting those things which are behind, and reaching forth unto those things which are before, I press toward the mark for the prize of the high calling of God in Christ Jesus." Philippians 3:13-14

"For this is the covenant that I will make with the house of Israel after those days, says the Lord; I will put My laws into their mind, and write them in their hearts: and I will be to them a God, and they shall be to Me a people." Hebrews 8:10

Dear Child,

Repentance is a great and powerful gift to be used continually. Those who follow closely with Me recognize their hopelessly sinful nature and rejoice in My ability to completely forgive and cleanse confessed sin. They value the cross and My work above all earthly gifts and powers. They recognize their dependence on Me continually and feel secure and protected in My love. This gives them joy above others and a life adventure beyond their expectations. They're humble, ready to serve and enjoy Me continually.

"If we confess our sins, He is faithful and just to forgive us our sins, and to cleanse us from all unrighteousness." I John 1:9

"You have loved righteousness and hated iniquity; therefore, God, even your God, has anointed you with the oil of gladness above your fellows." Hebrews 1:9

Dear Child,

I hold you close. Have mercy on your sins and failures. I do not judge you harshly, nor do your friends. Accept the seasons; as I turn the earth, so I turn your life experiences. When I seek to shed deeper sins, it seems lonely and darker in your life, but be of good cheer. Yield, rest and be patient for My good and glorious outcomes. Sorrow is indeed replaced by joy in a new, higher morning light. Believe that My intentions for you are always good and for My highest, loving purposes.

"To everything there is a season,
and a time to every purpose under the heaven." Ecclesiastes 3:1

"...weeping may endure for a night, but joy comes in the morning."
Psalm 30:5

Dear Child,

Like Mary of old, you've chosen the way of being close to Me, desiring to learn of Me and what I desire. I desire inner truth, the willingness to become whom I created you to be-My faithful, obedient, joyful child. In this season, we're going deeper; deep is calling to deep. There's pain in seeing the extent of human sin. There's sorrow when you see the extent of human suffering. Only in this can you truly be a helpful, healing servant, without deception, yet completely certain that I and My truth are the hope and answer to all human needs and suffering.

Jesus said, *"But one thing is needful: and Mary has chosen that good*
part, which shall not be taken away from her." Luke 10:42

"Behold, You desire truth in the inward parts: and in the hidden part
You shall make me to know wisdom." Psalm 51:6

Dear Child,

Waiting on Me is not always pleasant for you. Sometimes the wait is longer than expected, but that's when I want perseverance, faith, and patience to grow. Much must occur in the unseen while I am ordering answers to prayers and hopes. Everyone has their experiences of loss and pain as they want to understand their lives. All have a purpose and priority. My best is offered to My children as they learn to know Me and My laws by My Spirit.

"Knowing this, that the trying of your faith works patience.
But let patience have her perfect work,
that you may be perfect and entire, wanting nothing."
James 1:3-4

"The law of the Lord is perfect; converting the soul:
the testimony of the Lord is sure, making wise the simple.
The statutes of the Lord are right, rejoicing the heart:
the commandment of the Lord is pure, enlightening the eyes."
Psalm 19:7-8

My Dear Child,

I understand the pressures that oppose you and the wrong thinking that comes against you. I see it all, and I recognize the plots of your evil enemy and his tools. My answer is to listen closely to Me and rebuke the devil again and again. I give you My good, life-giving thoughts. Be especially alert and defensive when you are weary and burdened or ill. I come as you call. I rescue, save and heal.

"And Jesus rebuked the devil; And he departed out of him..."
Matthew 17:18

"As for me, I will call upon God; and the Lord shall save me."
Psalm 55:16

Dear Child,

Yes, by the measure of your love is your capacity to be able to suffer. Many have endured great suffering and triumphed through the ages because they knew the surety of My love for them and others. I, too, feel the suffering of My children and am comforted when they share mine. The mystery of suffering is that it must be experienced for My glory to dawn on humanity. All growth requires some type or degree of suffering. Out of sorrow comes My great joy if it is needed and embraced.

"For as the sufferings of Christ abound in us, so our consolation also abounds by Christ." II Corinthians 1:5

"That you might walk worthy of the Lord unto all pleasing, being fruitful in every good work, and increasing in the knowledge of God; strengthened with all might, according to His glorious power, unto all patience and longsuffering with joyfulness" Colossians 1:10-11

Dear Child,

At this time, you cannot grasp the perfection that I am. In eternity, you shall be able to understand yourself and your life story as I do. There will be wonders to contemplate endlessly. Much that you cannot see or understand now will be clear and meaningful. You can appreciate Me and My ways in freshness and depth. You will see how I accomplished My purposes on earth. You can recognize the great value, love, and care I lavish on My children. Let this give you peace and contentment now, and encourage all to receive Me for themselves.

"Can you by searching find out God? Can you find out the Almighty unto perfection?" Job 11:7

"As for God, His way is perfect..." Psalm 18:30

Dear Child,

I said, Suffer the little children to come unto Me. The experiences of early life go the deepest in children. They influence deeply, even if not remembered. I desire to meet their quest to understand all that they find happening. They have a longing for love and acceptance from Me from whom they've originated. I desire others to meet their needs on earth willingly and joyfully. Be one who draws the children to Me.

Jesus said, "...Suffer the little children to come unto Me, and forbid them not: for of such is the Kingdom of God. Verily I say unto you, Whosoever shall not receive the Kingdom of God as a little child, he shall not enter therein." Mark 10:14-15

"When my father and my mother forsake me, then the Lord will take me up." Psalm 27:10

My Dear Child,

Be kind to yourself. Continue to seek meaning and purpose through me, My Kingdom, and My people as they exist worldwide. Remain in contact and prayer for those I bring to you or your thoughts. There is much to keep you involved, growing, and interested. Let the cultural pursuits of the world pass by. These are of the sad, empty lives of those longing to be filled and happy in the ever changing lusts of man. I offer the real, the best, My very Self.

"Love not the world, neither the things that are in the world. If any man love the world, the love of the Father is not in him. For all that is in the world, the lust of the flesh, and the lust of the eyes, and the pride of life, is not of the Father, but is of the world. And the world passes away, and the lust thereof: but he that does the will of God, abides forever." I John 2:15-17

"But covet earnestly the best gifts: and yet show I unto you a more excellent way." I Corinthians 12:31

Dear Child,

There are many kinds of miracles. There is the word in season that immediately brings My light of revelation, answers, and solutions. Thereby I open blind eyes and closed hearts to My real presence and love. Often, this brings a needed and hoped-for healing that can be miraculous. Much of what is called sickness has roots in bondage to wrong thinking, beliefs, and lies. All behavior stems from man's thinking which needs to change for healing and transformation to occur.

"He sent His word, and healed them,
and delivered them from their destructions." Psalm 107:20

"And be not conformed to this world: but be transformed
by the renewing of your mind, that you may prove what is0
that good, and acceptable, and perfect, will of God." Romans 12:2

Dear Child,

Because you have learned repeatedly to mistrust others and draw away from them, I must remove this pattern from your mind to transfer steadfast trust to Myself. Love must overcome fear and self-protection. Your enemy would want you to build unhealthy walls that limit your life and could be used to attract inappropriate relationships. Remind yourself that I am always with you. I am always leading you to good, and I always love you. Go forward with My courage, trust, and compassionate love for yourself and others. I am your protection and future.

"There is no fear in love; but perfect love casts out fear..." I John 4:18

"Be sober, be vigilant; because your adversary the devil,
as a roaring lion, walks about, seeking whom he may devour:
Whom resist steadfast in the faith, knowing that the same afflictions
are accomplished in you brethren that are in the world." I Peter 5;8-9

Dear Child,

Calm yourself, and take My peace around you as a mantle. Settle all your wandering, anxious thoughts, and meditate on My power and virtue. I did not design you to take on extensive concerns and worry. Rest in your human limitations, be My child, expecting My help. Come to Me and find the rest for your body and soul. I protect My children from that which is too much for them to bear. I am an overseeing, shielding Father.

Jesus said, "Come unto Me, all you that labor and are heavy laden, and I will give you rest. Take My yoke upon you, and learn of Me; for I am meek and lowly in heart: and you shall find rest unto your souls. For My yoke is easy, and My burden is light." Matthew 11:28-30

"But You, O Lord, are a shield for me; my glory, and the lifter up of my head. I cried unto the Lord with my voice, and He heard me out of His holy hill." Psalm 3:3-4

Dear Child,

To the matter of sowing and reaping, there is a depth that only I comprehend. You see your life as a separate individual entity. I see your life as very much intricately woven into the whole fabric of My universe. You see circumstances that seem unexplainable. I see a creation that must experience the struggle to grow into the knowledge of Me, its Creator. These struggles and conflicts all have meaning and purpose. I do My part continually to reveal My character and care. I am complete love.

"Be not deceived; God is not mocked: for whatsoever a man sows, that shall he also reap. For he that sows to his flesh shall of the flesh reap corruption; but he that sows to the Spirit shall of the Spirit reap life everlasting." Galatians 6:7-8

"But grow in grace, and in the knowledge of our Lord and Savior Jesus Christ. To Him be glory both now and forever. Amen." II Peter 3:18

Dear Child,

Waiting upon Me means certainty in your heart that I hear, see, and am at work. Resting, breathing deeply of My presence brings joy in today. Remember, today is all you can experience, and I desire you not to miss it. Be sure I have forgiven your past sins and will forgive all those of today and tomorrow when you ask Me. Notice the concentration of children at play. This is what I desire for you; concentration on My nature, My thoughts, My work, My justice. This brings lasting, deep joy to My children.

"For in Him we live, and move, and have our being..." Acts 17:28

"Set your affection on things above, not on things on the earth."
Colossians 3:2

Dear Child,

You can follow Me outside of yourself into My timelessness. Quietness practiced will make the way to hear and communicate with Me. Today, your world is filled with noise, and even the airwaves are polluted. Men's minds and senses are filled with distractions you need to rise above and reject. My mind is far greater and stronger and is always available to those genuinely searching with all their heart. I do not abandon My children. Be comforted in My Presence and My conversation. You are in the world for My good purposes, but you can choose not to be of the world. I provide the higher way to My higher places.

"For God has not called us unto uncleanness, but unto holiness."
I Thessalonians 4:7

"Love not the world, neither the things that are in the world.
If any man love the world, the love of the Father is not in hm."
I John 2:15

Dear Child,

Do not dwell on the works of the devil; the horror and degradation that is ever increasing. I came to destroy the works of the devil, and I have, and I continue to do so. These days, it seems he has free reign to deceive and destroy, but My power in My people will prevail and conquer all evil. Your part is to agree with Me in prayer and intercede; standing with and for others, and My good hand to protect and provide in what seems to you impossible situations. Take hold of hope in Me.

"...For this purpose the Son of God was manifested, that He might destroy the works of the devil." I John 3:8

"For whatsoever is born of God overcomes the world: and this is the victory that overcomes the world, even our faith." I John 5:4

Dear Child,

The treasure you have given and laid up for Me and others on earth is laid up for you in heaven. In eternity, you will experience the vast value of selflessness on earth. The sacrifices and self-denial will appear small in comparison to the rich investment you've made in My Kingdom and My work. Cheerful, willing service, generosity, and forgiving forbearance are the currency you'll find invested in heaven with eternal returns. Would that mankind understood and pursued Me with the passion they foolishly invest in life's mammon, and selfishness and competition against one another. Listen, My children.

Jesus said, "Lay not up for yourselves treasures upon earth, where moth and rust corrupts, and where thieves break through and steal. But lay up for yourselves treasures in heaven, where neither moth nor rust corrupts, and where thieves do not break through and steal: For where your treasure is, there will your heart be also. Matthew 6:19-21

Jesus said, "No man can serve two masters: for either he will hate the one, and love the other; or else he will hold to the one, and despise the other. You cannot serve God and mammon." Matthew 6:24

Dear Child,

I can say, "Well done, My child," when others may not see much of anything done. A day of sweet, comforting fellowship between us does us both good! Your intercessions and appreciative, thankful thoughts for others are of much value and accomplishment that only I may know and recognize. I am the fathering God who keeps His children, and I use you to bring My power to earth. Well done, serving one.

Jesus said, " *His lord said unto him,*
Well done, good and faithful servant;
you have been faithful over a few things,
I will make you ruler over many things: enter into the joy of your lord. "
Matthew 25:23

"The Lord is your keeper…" Psalm 121:5

Dear Child,

Have I not made you more than a conqueror by My Spirit in you? Do not think of yourself in any way less. I've formed you year by year to My vision, My original design. Don't question or compare My design with another. Rejoice and stay glad that your life and personality are usable by Me as none other could be. Continue to call upon Me in every need. My resources are vast and unlimited. See My overcoming power and truth prevail always. Eternity with Me is awaiting and is your sure reward.

"No, in all these things we are more than conquerors
through Him that loved us." Romans 8:37

" He shall call upon Me, and I will answer him:
I will be with him in trouble; I will deliver him, and honor him. "
Psalm 91:15

Dear Child,

Be faithful to that which I have called you. Only I see the results and the true needs of those I desire you to show Myself and My love to. Seek Me and not human solutions. Pain and suffering are inevitable in your world. You must defer these to me and not carry them and sorrow for others excessively. Be resilient as a child, focused on this present moment with Me. Your intellect and emotions need to follow My Spirit. This can be learned and enjoyed. I say, be of good cheer.

Jesus said, "...Be faithful unto death, and I will give you a crown of life." Revelation 2:10

Jesus said, "These things I have spoken to you, that in Me you might have peace. In the world you shall have tribulation: but be of good cheer; I have overcome the world." John 16:33

Dear Child,

Enjoy the ever-changing scene on earth, knowing behind it all is My unchanging Self. See My principles at work, and experience My mighty, majestic power and glory. I am the power and glory forever. I hear your longing for people, nations, and the world to be restored to relationship with Me, their Creator. This longing originates from My heart. Find comfort in our unified purpose and work. Remain in a life of simplicity with your eyes on the purpose, and enjoy greatly being a small part of My redeeming, loving plan. Press on.

"My lips shall utter praise, when You have taught me Your statutes. My tongue shall speak of Your Word: for all Your commandments are righteousness." Psalm 119:171-172

Jesus said, "...For yours is the Kingdom, and the power, and the glory, for ever. Amen." Matthew 6:13

Dear Child,

Receive My peace. Allow Me to hold you close. There's no need to analyze and cast about for reasons, symbols, and solutions in every situation. I am in charge. You're not managing everything, filling in every lack, anticipating every need. Your intentions are good, but you need to rest in your role of waiting upon Me in peace. Only I understand all persons and situations, and I am already guiding the willing, gently, slowly, lovingly.

"And the peace of God, which passes all understanding, shall keep your hearts and minds through Christ Jesus." Philippians 4:7

"With Him is wisdom and strength, He has counsel and understanding." Job 12:13

Dear Child,

Tell others simply what I mean to your life. There's no need to hide your close, full relationship with Me. Many are lonely, empty, and desperate for meaning and help. Humbly, gently extend My cool, living water as you go about your days. Earnestly look into the eyes of people, and see the searching, the hopelessness. I am with you to respond in a way that will reveal My reality and love. Out of what is given to you abundantly, give! My children do not lack.

Jesus said, "…If any man thirst, let him come unto Me, and drink. He that believes on Me, as the scripture has said, out of his belly shall flow rivers of living water." John 7:37-38

Jesus said, "…Freely you have received, freely give." Matthew 10:8

My Child,

Do not fear, be anxious or try to look too far into the future. I already have your future in mind, and all is well. Enjoy all your moments of life close to Me today. Delight yourself in the interactions of every day with whomever I place before you. Look beyond who they appear to be, to the treasure each is to Me, and the importance they have in My plan. Some are to teach you, some are for your ministry and care, and some to purely enjoy. I think of everything you require. Be a good receiver, servant, and student.

"My times are in your hand..." Psalm 31:15

"While we look not at the things which are seen, but at the things which are not seen: for the things which are seen are temporal; but the things which are not seen are eternal." II Corinthians 4:18

Dear Child,

"Hallelujah, for the Lord our God the Almighty reigns." These are words heard in heaven and true. The gift of righteousness brings the gift of full, true living. There is no other way. Knowing Me is an experience of endless wonder, richness, and joy. For this, you were created and intended. Think on this, and allow all lesser concerns and desires to fade away. Many are blinded by their greed, selfishness, and small-mindedness. I desire the completeness and satisfaction of knowing Me and My true purpose and riches for My children. Be filled with My Spirit in your temple of joyfulness.

Jesus said, "...I am the way, the truth, and the life: no man comes unto the Father, but by Me." John 14:6

"For in Him dwells all the fullness of the Godhead bodily. And you are complete in Him, which is the head of all principality and power." Colossians 2:9-10

Dear Child,

What your eyes see can be a distraction or a Divine revelation. I desire your spiritual eyes to be open to what I show you and essential for My transforming work. You have noticed multitudes looking outwardly for identity, security, belonging. Over the world, there is now a mass traveling to and fro, searching to fulfill this emptiness within. This ultimate peace, joy, and security can only be found in close communion with Me, your Creator. Share your story with the lost, lonely searchers that they may find their home in Me and My goodness to them.

Jesus said, *"But blessed are your eyes, for they see: and your ears, for they hear."* Matthew 13:16

"But you O Daniel, shut up the words, and seal the book, even to the time of the end: many shall run to and fro, and knowledge shall be increased." Daniel 12:4

Be of good cheer, My Child.

You're following close. Leave results to My infinite wisdom, knowledge, and justice. Am I not beautifully perfect? I do not condemn you for your imperfections and sins forgiven, but learn from the consequences and turn to Me as a corrected child. Be embraced and start afresh. Fasting will help you with self-reflection, a revelation of Me and My way of control by My Spirit. You belong to Me, My family, My Kingdom. Your behavior must come into this way.

"There is therefore now no condemnation to them which are in Christ Jesus, who walk not after the flesh, but after the Spirit." Romans 8:1

Jesus said, *"...When you fast, be not, as the hypocrites, of a sad countenance..."* Matthew 6:16

Dear Child,

Waiting upon Me is not aimless. I am always revealing Myself and My thoughts to you. Keep your inner eyes seeing the signs and wonders all around you, everywhere. Choose the tree of life and its healing leaves. I hear and understand your prayers and longings. I satisfy them. I embrace, affirm and comfort you. Receive it all without doubt of your worth to Me. I am enjoying the story of your abundant life, and I am a rewarder of them that seek, love, and ask, not only for yourself but for many others. You come after My heart of compassion. It is I who have given you the gift of mercy. In Me, you find the perfect justice your heart longs for.

Jesus said,
"...To him that overcomes
will I give to eat of the tree of life,
which is in the midst of the paradise of God."
Revelation 2:7

"For He satisfies the longing soul,
and fills the hungry soul with goodness."
Psalm 107:9

Winter

Dear Child,

Am I not all-powerful, everywhere present and available? Agree for My highest will for your land and leaders. Only I can know the outcome of those who stand for My righteousness. Circumstances may appear dim, but the important work is being achieved in the secret place with Me. Yes, I desire truth in the inward parts. I am the God of justice and mercy. I wait for man to choose Me willingly and gladly. Then, My order prevails.

"Righteousness exalts a nation: but sin is a reproach to any people."
Proverbs 14:34

"...choose you this day whom you will serve...
but as for me and my house, we will serve the Lord." Joshua 24:15

Dear Child,

All your days are in My hands, planned and awaiting your participation and choices. I set the stage and season, and your part is to respond. I am a Godly Father of order and good purpose. Your life is not a series of random occurrences. I know each of My children intimately and desire them to long to know Me intimately. What a lovely communion we can continually enjoy. In a close, authentic relationship, I give individual, personal leadership to satisfy your heart. I alone can bring you to a complete, awake experience of who I created you to be. Receive Me, and receive your heart's desires fulfilled.

"The steps of a good man are ordered by the Lord: and he delights in His way. Though he fall; he shall not be utterly cast down: for the Lord upholds him with His hand." Psalm 37:23-24

"But as many as received him, to them gave he power to become the sons of God, even to them that believe on his name:" John 1:12

Dear Child,

I understand the suffering and effort of keeping to your vows and responsibilities. Yet, I hold you to these vows and commitments. Many fail to see the consequences and destructiveness of breaking their vows to Me. Much of what pains you and Me and others is a result of unfaithfulness. I am close and available when you call upon Me for strength to continue and do well. A true servant needs to lay aside selfishness and pride. Remember, I give unlimited grace to the humble. I also honor and reward those who honor Me and are faithful to their commitments.

"Praise waits for You, O God, in Sion:
and unto You shall the vow be performed." Psalm 65:1

Jesus said, *"If any man serve Me, let him follow Me;*
and where I am, there shall also My servant be:
if any man serve Me, him will My Father honor." John 12:26

Yes, My child,

Confusion does appear to reign in much of the world, and man's thinking seems so limited to you. Do not let your heart be troubled. Through centuries, religions have obscured My simple truths and overlaid them with burdensome expectations and traditions. I came to clear up the confusion and left My Spirit to continue revealing the simplicity of following Me. Now, there is a significant acceleration of the gospel news in the earth. Be encouraged that all confusion will disappear when I appear again. Press on in making Me known in your life.

"For God is not the author of confusion, but of peace,
as in all churches of the saints." I Corinthians 14:33

Jesus said, *"And then shall they see the Son of man*
coming in the clouds with great power and glory." Mark 13:26

Dear Child,

There is no need to seek after the honor and praise of men. I bestow these upon those who honor Me and live for My Kingdom and Me. I am holding your hand with My right hand of righteousness, leading you on My narrow path of victory over your sinful self. This is sufficient for your well-being and fruitfulness. Continue to obey My instructions day by day with no care for man's approval. Know assuredly, that it is I alone who has called you to serve Me and others in the work of healing, prophesy, and going to those who are lost.

"But he is a Jew, which is one inwardly;
and circumcision is that of the heart, in the spirit, and not in the letter;
whose praise is not of men, but of God." Romans 2:29

"I the Lord have called you in righteousness, and will hold your hand,
and will keep you, and give you for a covenant of the people,
a light of the Gentiles." Isaiah 42:6

Dear Child,

Covet to prophesy. Keep sharply tuned to My voice to reveal the wisdom, knowledge, and thoughts only I know. I want to reveal Myself in this way to those who do not believe in Me. Even the miraculous can take place because I give words of life to those in need. Take courage to obey as I direct in the supernatural gifts. Put aside all fear of man and appearing foolish or humiliated. Life with Me is always more and more humbling. As I say, deny yourself and follow where I lead.

"Wherefore, brethren, covet to prophesy,
and forbid not to speak with tongues." I Corinthians 14:39

"The fear of man brings a snare:
but whoso puts his trust in the Lord shall be safe." Proverbs 29:25

Dear Child,

You have My love given to you. It's a love willing to endure and even suffer for righteousness; love that expects nothing for itself, only wanting others to see and know Me for themselves. You are often alone and misunderstood as you must stand back and let situations be until I can work My will. You are in a place where we can meet eye to eye in understanding. This pleases Me. Have less concern about displeasing others in your imperfections. I came to seek and save the lost. As you were once lost, enjoy helping others come to Me.

"Charity suffers long and is kind..." I Corinthians 13:4

Jesus said, "For the Son of Man has come to seek and to save that which was lost." Luke 19:10

Dear Child,

Though it seems and appears impossible to many, I am indeed ordering, controlling the universe I created. Remember, I created you for companionship and a knowing relationship with Myself. Therefore, I allowed you to think, reflect and choose. Much of what happens on earth is grievous to me as a loving Father. Mankind has long forgotten who they are and why I created them. I sent My Son to cause them to remember where they came from and where they must return It was My reclaiming love that allowed His sacrifice. I sent My most precious gift. My heart longs to see Him received in fullness and understanding.

"You are worthy, O Lord, to receive glory and honor and power: for You have created all things, and for Your pleasure they are and were created." Revelation 4:11

"...He that receives Me, receives Him that sent Me." John 13:20

Dear Child,

Yes, let My peace cover your heart and protect your thoughts. I am the Great Sustainer. You can relax and be comforted at home with Me. I am not pressuring you to to be about doing and serving continually. There are times to withdraw, observe and be thankful. I speak to you often to take rest, as I did while on earth. There will always be much to trouble your soul and demand attention. Above all, I am your protecting, wise Father who will guide you. Your part is to hear continually, obey and rejoice.

"You will keep him in perfect peace, whose mind is stayed on You: because he trusts in You." Isaiah 26:3

"I will greatly rejoice in the Lord, my soul shall be joyful in My God; for He has clothed me with the garments of salvation, He has covered me with the robe of righteousness..." Isaiah 61:10

My Dear Child,

I hear the cry of your heart for strength to bear with the pain of others. I give you a taste of My love and mercy for the needs of the world. Your joy must stem from My comfort, always available with hope in Me. Receive a deeper revelation of My love as you see Me amidst life's sorrows. I, the Man of Sorrows, unfailing in My love for the earth, am always available to whosoever calls on Me. Do not withdraw from life's sorrows, but use them as an opportunity to draw close to Me and receive My strength, wisdom, and comfort to give.

"He is despised and rejected of men; a man of sorrows, and acquainted with grief..." Isaiah 53:3

"...the joy of the Lord is your strength." Nehemiah 8:10

Dear Child,

Yes, I do like a dialogue with My children. I am the great, listening Father you need. Just as you enjoy the confidence of others and their response to your heart, I too enjoy that you come to Me continually in expectation. I am interested in, and like you to know that I care about, all the details of your life. Your reliance on and trust in Me and My will, creates steadfastness, security, strength to your life and your whole being. Savor the rich life with Me as Divine Companion, counseling Father.

"Now I know that the Lord saves His anointed;
He will hear him from His holy heaven
with the saving strength of His right hand." Psalm 20:6

"...and His Name shall be called Wonderful, Counsellor,
The Mighty God, the Everlasting Father,
The Price of Peace." Isaiah 9:6

Dear Child,

Now I am calling out across the world to My friends, to come closer, hear what I have to say and show you; be about My work. Release your efforts to lesser pursuits and honors. Let go of the world's pressure to consume and grasp. See the true nature and state of these times. Each has a place of speaking and demonstrating My truth and love. Work now while you can to bring many to peace with me and faith in My Words. Humble obedience in the small, ordinary things is all that is required.

"But it is good for me to draw near to God: I have put my trust in the
Lord God, that I may declare all Your works." Psalm 73:28

Jesus said, *"I must work the works of Him that sent me, while it is day:*
the night comes, when no man can work." John 9:4

Dear Child,

Yes, I am the God of the new, the everchanging newness. I am always restoring the old and transforming what is to what I have in mind. Therefore, be open in your mind and emotions to Me afresh daily. There's no boredom nor dull moments in a life close to Me. I make you rich in the real treasures of wisdom, compassion, understanding, and love as you experience your life in Me. There is no end to My wondrous giving and revelation. Laugh and be merry with Me.

"Behold, I will do a new thing; now it shall spring forth; shall you not know it? I will even make a way in the wilderness, and rivers in the desert." Isaiah 43:19

"...he that is of a merry heart has a continual feast." Proverbs 15:15

Dear Child,

Yes, rejoice evermore as I reveal My victory in your life. There is none other. The fruit of living in Me is glorious to experience and give away. Man has many devices and solutions, but none give the lasting peace, security, joy, and order that My redeeming blood provides. I so loved the world greatly that I gave My best and most precious Son to be the answer for all earth's troubles. Yes, I AM speaks to those who will hear and trust and obey, to the victorious life I have planned.

"But thanks be to God, which gives us the victory through our Lord Jesus Christ." I Corinthians 15:57

"And God said to Moses, I AM that I AM....." Exodus 3:14

Dear Child,

Many are lost, searching without hope or direction for their rightful place in life. They are desperate to find the peace that only comes from My Spirit alive in them. Therefore, you are appointed as a sign, pointing the way to salvation and eternal life. Entry into My Kingdom must have a beginning, an entrance. I am that Door, and you are a doorkeeper on the watch for the wanderers. Yes, there's a sadness as you view the condition of the lost and broken; but take heart, as you know well how I, the Mender, can heal and restore anything.

Jesus said, *"I am the door: by Me if any man enter in, he shall be saved, and shall go in and out, and find pasture."* John 10:9

"...I had rather be a doorkeeper in the house of my God, than to dwell in the tents of wickedness." Psalm 84:10

Dear Child,

No person is insignificant. I love and value each one. All are of My creation, no matter their condition. I grieve for the pain of sin's consequences and the environment of rejection and blindness often caused by it. All this does not change the worth I place on My creation and the good purposes I always intend. Share My pity, and be available to comfort as I comfort and help. Stay open and teachable to the big world picture where I want to use you. Even the smallest prayer, kindest thought, or deed can have extensive help and My good impact. Share My care for the lowly, needy, and overlooked ones.

"Blessed be God, even the Father of our Lord Jesus Christ, the Father of mercies, and the God of all comfort; Who comforts us in all our tribulation, that we may be able to comfort them which are in any trouble, by the comfort wherewith we ourselves are comforted of God." II Corinthians 1:3-4

"Though the Lord is high, He yet respects the lowly" Psalm 138:6

Dear Child,

I am the sunshine, the light of your life, shining through you. Keep the clouds away. Stay as a sweet, open, trusting child. I determine your life by what's on the inside. The attitude of your heart and your attention towards Me are more important than what is displayed externally. My Spirit directs you to all that will bring life: green, fresh, multiplying life. Even in the winter months, you can have flourishing growth in the sunshine of My truth. Don't compare yourself to the externals, but leave them to Me. Stay sweet and submitted.

*"He that trusts in his riches shall fall:
but the righteous shall flourish as a branch." Proverbs 11:28*

*"For we dare not make ourselves of the number, or compare ourselves
with some that commend themselves...." II Corinthians 10:12*

Dear Child,

Yes, I am the healer over all the world. I cause the newness of life and mend that which is broken or torn. I grieve for all the destruction you see in the world. I am allowing it to witness the attempts of man to live and choose his own way, hoping he will turn to My Way and Me. Those who know and love Me are called to be My healing laborers and peacemakers. Be encouraged that My restoring love and power are with you as you follow My lead, to see people, families and nations restored to Me.

*"I have taught you in the way of wisdom; I have led you in right paths."
Proverbs 4:11*

*Jesus said, "Blessed are the peacemakers:
for they shall be called the children of God." Matthew 5:9*

Dear Child,

Yes, the deep snow calls you into quiet rest. As you release all the racing thoughts and concerns to Me, you'll find a space I will fill with just being in My peaceful Presence. You'll be able to realize how little of your life is under your control, and you can trust all into My wise hands. What I place upon your path has so much more meaning and purpose than you can imagine. You do not want to miss My best by rushing past in pursuit of less, and even, perhaps, what is not to your benefit. Quietly meditate on My Word and your life's drama in peace.

"He makes me to lie down in green pastures:
He leads me beside the still waters." Psalm 23:2

"I will meditate in Your precepts, and have respect unto Your ways."
Psalm 119:15

Dear Child,

All is in perfect order in My Kingdom. Holiness is the perfect order and balance of all I do, say, and think. All your ideas of what is unseen, such as love, joy, peace, justice, originate in My Mind, the Mind Of Christ. You can see and discern the outcome of these ideas manifesting on earth. Many imagine these come from themselves and are under their control. In childlike humility, it becomes clear that all these good gifts and ideas are from above. Therefore, they can be experienced and enjoyed freely, generously, and divinely.

"Many, O Lord My God, are Your wonderful works which You have
done, and Your thoughts which are to us-ward: they cannot be reckoned
up in order unto You: if I would declare and speak of them,
they are more than can be numbered." Psalm 40:5

"But seek you first the Kingdom of God, and His righteousness; and all
these things shall be added unto you." Matthew 6:33

Dear Child,

When I say I am with you, even unto the end of the world, I mean just that. There's no need to allow fear to enter your life. Fear can cause you to pursue security from elsewhere besides from Me. I am your Father of right plans and destiny. Your life in My secret place is safe and. All that is needed by you has already been prepared. I am most pleased when your trust goes ahead to produce true peace and joy in you and is then made available to others. I created all for your enjoyment and wondrous surveillance of My Kingdom and Me. As a good Father, I am ever watchful, protecting, and providing for you. Abide in Me as I embrace you.

Jesus said, *"...I am with you always, even unto the end of the world."*
Matthew 28:20

Jesus said, *"Fear not, little flock; for it is your Father's good pleasure to give you the Kingdom." Luke 12:32*

Dear Child of Mine,

Most profoundly, you recognize how hardship and long-suffering fulfill a need in one's growth and knowledge of Me. If I allow these times of pressing, it is to remove from your character whatever hinders your growth in My goodness. Allow these times to press you to My heart where you will receive the actual, true comfort of belonging to Me. From that will come greater receptivity to all you need in your journey to eternity, your authentic home place.

"That you might walk worthy of the Lord unto all pleasing, being fruitful in every good work, and increasing in the knowledge of God; Strengthened with all might, according to His glorious power, unto all patience and long suffering with joyfulness." Colossians 1:10-11

"You therefore endure hardness, as a good soldier of Jesus Christ."
II Timothy 2:3

Dear Child,

Be comforted and assured that My Presence is all around you, and My Spirit fills you. Be sure of My care as you are deeply engaged in caring for, understanding, and responding to many around you. I receive your adoration, your heart's cry for My help, and your unfailing belief that I hear and will be all you need. This is My life-giving flow to My children; always available, never failing. In this special season of rejoicing in My best gift, My perfect Son, know that I will never fail you in all seasons. Let your heart sing My praises for all to hear.

"Let us come before His Presence with thanksgiving,
and make a joyful noise unto Him with psalms." Psalm 95:2

"For unto us a child is born, unto us a Son is given…" Isaiah 9:6

Dear Child,

Concerning My birth as a babe on earth, I came to show the great value I place on human life, marriage, and family. These were created by Me, and ordained as My plan for humanity. I ordered life by My life, as an example of My eternal pattern. I created all by My Word, and each new life is a seed of hope for humanity. Much would corrupt life on earth, but My Word still holds, and I will always triumph in some way. There's a mystery in all My ways.

"And she brought forth her first born Son,
and wrapped Him in swaddling clothes, and laid Him in a manger;
because there was no room for them in the inn." Luke 2:7

"I have made the earth, and created man upon it:
I, even My hands, have stretched out the heavens,
and all their host have I commanded."
Isaiah 45:12

Dear Child,

What I give, I give entirely, beautifully. I gave My Son ultimately as a beautiful gift. I am perfection, and My gifts are good and perfect. I delight in giving My children gifts. For those who are full of thanksgiving, My gifts multiply. My followers themselves become gifts. They live to give, as I do, with no manipulation nor control. They know how freely they have been given, and they give freely. They recognize the joy and adventure of giving and serving in My Name. Go, receive, and give liberally.

"Every good and every perfect gift is from above, and comes down from the Father of lights, with whom is no variableness, neither shadow of turning." James 1:17

Jesus said, "...It is more blessed to give than to receive." Acts 20:35

Dear Child,

Yes, I am Immanuel with you, touching you with My Spirit of comfort, warming, and cheering you. I am the gift that never changes. I am leading in all the details of your life and delight to do good through you. Be refreshed, My child, and help to refresh others. You feel My compassion for the hurting ones, and My power of love motivates you to alleviate pain, and bring My Good News, the Gospel of Peace, to earth. Shine on for Me, and let your heart be glad.

"Therefore the Lord Himself shall give you a sign; Behold, a virgin shall conceive, and bear a Son, and shall call His Name Immanuel." Isaiah 7:14

Jesus said, "And this Gospel of the Kingdom shall be preached in all the world for a witness unto all nations; and then shall the end come." Matthew 24:14

Dear Child,

Adoration of Me and My Kingdom coming does not happen easily to the natural man. For this reason, I said, "You must be born again." I didn't come to make you a better person, but to make you a new creation. All things become new when your spirit awakens to Mine. Don't waste time in regrets for the time of life lived away from Me. Hold even closer to Me now, and let your adoration flow out to Me so all can see a transformed life.

Jesus said, "...Truly, truly, I say unto you, Except a man be born of water and of the Spirit, he cannot enter into the Kingdom of God." John 3:5

"Therefore if any man be in Christ, he is a new creature: old things are passed away; behold, all things are become new." II Corinthians 5:17

Dear Child,

All the lights, music, and gifts are a dim reflection of what exists, awaiting you in eternity. Those who've glimpsed heaven have inadequate words to describe My heavenly realm. Man's creative desires stem from his search for the ultimate glory, beauty, and perfection of Me. I have designed you in this way, in My image, wanting the lost unity we once had. Receive My peace, order, and security as I lead--no need for wearying, anxious pressure.

In heaven, "...the city had no need of the sun, neither of the moon, to shine in it: for the glory of God did lighten it, and the Lamb is the light thereof." Revelation 21:23

"For you were as sheep going astray; but are now returned unto the Shepherd and Bishop of your souls." I Peter 2:25

Dear Child,

Have I not created you with multiple senses, enabling you to enjoy being alive in the world of endless delights? But these delights are intended to be experienced in My timing, order, and measure. No man can live unto themself and thrive. My creation works together in a balanced purpose as I intend. Only when you agree with Me does the working bring forth life and more life. Wisdom should be the outcome of a life lived under My care and direction. Anything else leads to sin, destruction, and death.

"For wisdom is better than rubies;
and all the things that may be desired are not to be compared to it."
Proverbs 8:11

"For the wages of sin is death; but the gift of God is eternal life through
Jesus Christ our Lord." Romans 6:23

Dear Child,

Many are remembering My birth on earth these days. I came into your darkness to make it possible for you to come into My light. I chose complete helplessness so you could completely experience My reality and power. Still, many do not recognize the great gift I still extend to them and the most valuable treasure I am. All that lifts the souls of mankind abounds today to speak of Me and My gifts. Brightness, shining fullness, joy, and music are all of Me, and speak without words all can understand.

Jesus said, "…I am the light of the world: he that follows Me shall not
walk in darkness, but shall have the light of life.' John 8:12

"But you, O Lord, are a shield for me; my glory,
and the lifter up of my head." Psalm 3:3

Dear Child,

All about you is My glorious handiwork and loving care. I cause the sun to shine and warm and nurture My people. I hear and enjoy the high praises of those who know Me and can recognize My gifts to men. Be comforted with your heart stayed on My nature and My unchanging love. Yes, there is much reaping of sorrow and fear on the earth, but I am not the author of this. O, if men would turn to Me, the One Living God, there would be peace on earth as I would have it in My Son the Redeemer.

"The heavens declare the glory of God; and the firmament shows His handiwork." Psalm 19:1

"And suddenly there was with the angel a multitude of the heavenly host praising God, and saying, Glory to God in the highest, and on earth peace, good will toward men." Luke 2:13-14

Dear Child,

Rest. This is a excellent way to begin a new year. Some are weary due to worry and fear of the unknown. Some are weary of merry-making to escape life's troubles. So, I say, as always, come to me for the true rest, comfort, and peace I alone offer. Everyone likes to be invited, welcomed, and prepared for. I am the author of this invitation, always waiting for one to choose me and choose life with me in My Kingdom, a place that does not disappoint. Begin a new year with hope in Me that will not disappoint.

Jesus said, "Come unto Me, all you that labor and are heavy laden, and I will give you rest." Matthew 11:28

"My soul, waits only upon God; for my expectation is from Him." Psalm 62:5

Dear Child,

Place and keep your focus on Me, even when others attempt to draw it to themselves and their wants. Distractions are endless and wearisome. They will try to fragment your peace and bring heaviness because you are not designed to be the savior of others. I am the light and give you my light which uplifts and does not weigh down. Remember how I often needed to draw away with My Father when I was on earth. Drawing away is not defeat. Acknowledge your human limitations and neediness. I am there with you to fill and affirm you, and My companionship will strengthen and bring My order and clarity to you.

"Heaviness in the heart of man makes it stoop:
but a good word makes it glad." Proverbs 12:25

"But God has chosen the foolish things of the world to confound the wise;
and God has chosen the weak things of the world to confound the things
which are mighty." I Corinthians 1:27

Dear Child,

I am an enlarging, expansive God. I am always revealing more and more of Myself to the hungry and seeking. It's My delight to see My children growing in the knowledge of and love for Me. I know only good will come from their maturing and joyful experiences with Me. Expansion and contraction are real patterns I use to teach and train My children. Yield to My infinite wisdom that works with perfect balance and love.

He has filled the hungry with good things;
and the rich He has sent empty away." Luke 1:53

"Lead me in Your truth, and teach me: for You are the God of my
salvation; on you do I wait all the day." Psalm 25:5

Dear Child,

Serving Me is not as serving the world for personal gain. Serving Me is as a servant. You learn to see the needs and opportunities of others as I see them. I am a personal Father. I formed My creation to interact with Me. Therefore, you labor with Me for the good of people and creation. There may be little or no recognition or great wealth resulting from your service, but you have My pleasure, companionship, and all My riches available to you. I know your needs and desires and meet them abundantly.

"Serve the Lord with gladness: come before His presence with singing.
Know that the Lord He is God: it is He that has made us,
and not we ourselves; we are His people, and the sheep of His pasture."
Psalm 100:2-3

Jesus said, *"...I am come that they might have life,*
and that they might have it more abundantly." John 10:10

Dear Child,

Yes, you see Me as clearly as you can from your side of heaven. Therefore, you are marked, called away from lesser pursuits. You've received the great gift of open eyes to My power, My plans, and My pain. I have made your life rich, richer than you know. I have more for you to experience yet, and more of My life to give to others. All are important, even seemingly small, insignificant details. Receive My peace in daily struggles; draw upon My strength, make Me known by your very life and being.

Jesus said, *"But blessed are your eyes, for they see: and your ears,*
for they hear." Matthew 13:16

"Riches and honor are with Me; yes, durable riches and righteousness.
My fruit is better than gold, yes, than fine gold; and
My revenue than choice silver." Proverbs 8:18-19

Dear Child,

Those who serve mammon would like you to envy them and emulate them. Gently turn from these temptations, and pray for the blinded, lost ones. There is no lack to My children and much joy in My provision and timing. Be about My work, and hold fast to My truth; My Word never changes. Indeed, I am an anchor to your soul in the strong winds that would try to blow you to empty riches. Stay thankful for all you have in your Father's House."

Jesus said, *"And lead us not into temptation, but deliver us from evil: For yours is the Kingdom, and the power, and the glory, for ever. Amen"* Matthew 6:13

Jesus said, *"...I must be about My Father's business."* Luke 2:49

Dear Child,

In your world, My true peace is a real treasure. Many try to manufacture their own peace and control their circumstances to try to maintain it. This is all in vain and always fruitless. My true peace is obtained in quite the opposite way. My peace must be received by a humble, teachable heart. My way is not to control and manage people but to give them the freedom to search, think, reflect and grow. As they recognize their true needs, I reveal Myself as the all-sufficient, ever available, forgiving Father. Then, lasting, sweet peace becomes a reality. It does truly pass your understanding and become a great treasure.

"Not that we are sufficient of ourselves to think anything as of ourselves; but our sufficiency is of God." II Corinthians 3:5

" And the peace of God, which passes all understanding, shall keep your hearts and minds through Christ Jesus." Philippians 4:7

Dear Child,

Hold steady and faithful where I've placed you, and resist the temptation to find an easier way and place. This is where the pruning happens, where you can expect more fruit. I do not promise ease and comfort at all times. These are the result of looking to Me for help, solutions, and persevering strength. I am after not only your ultimate destination in glory but that of the many your life effects. Yield to My instruction; gain the gold of wisdom and peace of a clear conscience.

"My son, despise not the chastening of the Lord; neither be weary of His correction: For whom the Lord loves He corrects; even as a Father the son in whom He delights." Proverbs 3:11-12

"Herein is My Father glorified, that you bear much fruit…" John 15:8

Dear Child,

As I use you, it is not the same as being useful. Each has a different placement and purpose. Some are in positions that appear nearly useless. I work in the unseen where much might be happening in one's life and seems useless--even a burden of responsibility to others. My purpose may be far different from what is valued in your world. My character is formed in pain to your nature and comes in individual sorts, usually unexpectedly. Remember, I am an overseeing Father. I know what the very best for My children is. Accept that I always have your growth in mind. Truly, I arrange seasons so that you go from glory to glory.

"To everything there is a season, and a time to every purpose under heaven." Ecclesiastes 3:1

"But we all, with open face beholding as in a glass the glory of the Lord, are changed into the same image from glory to glory, even as by the Spirit of the Lord." II Corinthians 3:18

Dear Child,

My peace is a precious gift that few experience consistently. It can be felt by those who lack it, thereby raising questions and need. For most, it is received after painfully casting about for help. Disappointments are My appointments. Extend a hand, an arm, or a shoulder to those who need Me and My peace. Stay gentle but firm in comforting the lost, confused, and hurting. They are everywhere around you. My arms are great enough for whosoever will come. Be the friend to others, as I am the Friend to you. Everything good comes from Me. Be generous as I am generous.

"The eternal God is your refuge, and underneath are the everlasting arms..." Deuteronomy 33:27

"And the scripture was fulfilled which said, Abraham believed God, and it was imputed unto him for righteousness: and he was called the Friend of God." James 2:23

Dear Child,

I've given you a merciful, nurturing heart. There must be a balance of trusting Me completely with this gift. I am not expecting you to take on responsibility for all the pain and needs you see and feel so much Therefore, pray at once for what you experience. Pray that My Spirit would take on this need and whether or not you should do anything about it. Prayer is so much more powerful than you know. I hear when you receive My heart on a matter. That gives special power to its right outcome. In all, I am Sovereign and want your close fellowship in agreement.

"Pray without ceasing." I Thessalonians 5:17

"Can two walk together, except they agree?" Amos 3:3

Dear Child,

I've spoken to you about rest. By this, I don't mean only sleep, but releasing anxiety about matters for which you pray. Lift these matters to Me as they press on your soul. Call My Name when concern for others tries to overwhelm you. I hear and draw closer to reinforce my peace and confidence that I know, understand, and am involved. My sensitive Spirit in you may alert you for prayer needs so you can join in the fight, but the battle is Mine. I hold the earth together, and you are not the controller. Rest in confidence in Me, your Heavenly Father.

"Because He has inclined His ear unto me, therefore will I call upon Him as long as I live." Psalm 116:2

"...the battle is the Lord's" I Samuel 17:47

Dear Child,

There is beauty and freedom from giving each new day's experiences to Me early on. See each waking morning as fresh with Me and all that I desire to walk in with you. This retards all weary thoughts and routine concerns. Be as a child, looking about for new wonders and delights. Relish My life energy in and around you and how I meet all your needs. See each life as part of your story leading on to glory. Truly, all you experience with Me is abundance made manifest. Rejoice and enjoy with thankfulness.

"My voice shall you hear in the morning, O Lord: in the morning will I direct my prayer unto You, and will look up." Psalm 5:3

"But My God shall supply all your need according to His riches in glory by Christ Jesus." Philippians 4:19

Dear Child,

Waiting upon Me is essential, not a cause for impatience. Open your eyes by My Spirit, and be delighted to see much is silently happening all around you. I am a dynamic God, always affecting life around you and My world. I want you also to be ever reflecting your experience to My character and Word. This gives you a rich inner life, as you expect, and you see Me at work continually. I neither slumber nor sleep; omniscient and omnipresent.

"...I meditate on all Your works; I muse on the work of Your hands."
Psalm 143:5

"Behold, He that keeps Israel shall neither slumber nor sleep."
Psalm 121:4

Dear Child,

Continually focus on My Word and Me to avoid the entanglements and fears from within and without. Analyzing and digging for reasons, answers, and hope, will not, in the end, bring My unconditional love to and from you. As a little child looks expectantly to parents, look to Me to shed the light you need in all your circumstances. My Word is sufficient to every need. Faith, hope, and charity can only be seen in behavior. I want to bring these forth abundantly and unmistakably. Be the calm channel for all good to flow through, without hindrances.

"Your Word is a lamp unto my feet, and a light unto my path."
Psalm 119:105

"And now abides faith, hope, charity, these three; but the greatest of these is charity." I Corinthians 13:13

Dear Child,

I affirm you, child. I have great compassion for you. I long to, and am, restoring what was lost and needed in your life. Your sufferings and lack have given you great sensitivity to the needs and pain of others. I use this merciful heart daily as you pray for and nurture and teach others. There's always more to learn as you fulfill your destiny. Be released from all shame and inferiority. I smile upon you with pleasure, delighting in the future I know is coming. Be a happy, grateful, receptive child. Receive, without a doubt, that this is My good will for you.

"...The Lord is gracious and full of compassion." Psalm 111:4

"And I will restore to you
the years that the locust has eaten..." Joel 2:25

Dear Child,

The invitation is always extended to whosoever will come. Come to Me willingly, readily, the first time, or every time your mind wanders or is drawn to temptation. There is self-discipline needed to win control over your thoughts. I give you the capacity to reason, to read, write, discern and choose, as the tools to help you grow towards Me and My Words of truth. The evil one tries to use My gifts for your and his selfish, evil purposes. But, My power, and your obedience and faith, defeat wrong and bring My righteousness in thoughts, words, and deeds. Rejoice in My victory!

Jesus said,
"The thief comes not, but for to steal, and to kill, and to destroy:
I am come that they might have life,
and that they might have it more abundantly." John 10:10

"For whatsoever is born of God overcomes the world: and this is the
victory that overcomes the world, even our faith." I John 5:4

Dear Child,

Do not fear the changing seasons of life, for every story, must have a beginning, plot, and conclusion. I am the great story maker. Enjoy every story life around you, learning and marveling at My knowledge and purposes. Delight in recognizing what you gained through your life experience, and gold will come from all you have been freed from and what has transformed you. Truly, My motive is always love and growth to holiness. Recognize the high value I place on every life.

"And even to your old age I am He;
and even to hoar hairs will I carry you:
I have made, and I will bear; even I will carry,
and will deliver you." Isaiah 46:4

"And a highway shall be there, and a way,
and it shall be called
The way of holiness…"
Isaiah 35:8

Dear Child,

Encourage yourself in My unchanging Words of life. Resist the pressure of your world to change the truth, and deny My Word to mankind and Me. I left nothing to man's selfish, dark willfulness. I am light and clear in what I say, with no room to waver. Trust that I have the power and glory to perform what I say, now and forever.

"…David encouraged himself in the Lord his God." I Samuel 30:6

Jesus said,
"For Yours is the Kingdom, and the power,
and the glory, for ever. Amen."
Matthew 6:13

Dear Child,

I give My children years, as many years as are needed to grow into My idea of who they are. This usually requires years, seasons, failures, much learning, and transformation. Time means nothing to Me. I am eternal and endless in mercy, grace, and patience. Often years are shortened to spare great suffering and unnecessary pain to others. However long or short, life in your world is a gift to be marveled at and enjoyed. To know Me is the needed element for a rich, full, Godly, meaningful, and generous life.

"So teach us to number our days,
that we may apply our hearts unto wisdom." Psalm 90:12

"Jesus Christ the same yesterday, and today and for ever."
Hebrews 13:8

Dear Child,

Look about you at the wealth of life necessities that I have provided. Untold lives have been sacrificed to enhance your life to make more and more blessings available to all mankind. Your response should be unspeakable gratitude to your Heavenly Father and seeing evidence of His eternal love and mercy to mankind. Recognize there's no need for greed, competition, and ruthless selfishness in mankind. All this, I came to forgive and transform. Be a participant in My giving, healing, saving work.

"For the earth is the Lord's, and the fullness thereof."
I Corinthians 10:26

Jesus said,
"For the Son of man is come to seek
and to save
that which was lost."
Luke 19:10

Dear Child,

Yes, blessed, or favored are you when others despitefully use you and say many lies against you. It is a sin to avoid truth out of pride and selfprotection, and worse, to use others harmfully to do so. You are blessed to share My sufferings. The reality and depth of human sinfulness and betrayal can only be recognized and faced by My redeemed children. True, deep, continual soul cleansing is only possible to those truly born-again children, undeceived about their continuous need for My grace, mercy, forgiveness, and love.

Jesus said, "But I say unto you which hear,
Love your enemies, do good to them which hate you.
Bless them that curse you, and pray for them which despitefully use you."
Luke 6:27-28

"Create in me a clean heart, O God; and renew a right spirit within me."
Psalm 51:10

Dear Child,

The prophetic spirit of Elijah is speaking today to whomsoever will listen. He is revealing the deep mysteries of the gospel and My grace. As I am revealed to them for my purposes, many are shocked and astounded. They wonder at the extreme blindness of mankind, and are pained at the consequences that can be expected. All these are motivated to obey Me and do what they can to serve Me. True belief and trust in My Word and character and Kingdom to come results in serving with gladness.

"And Jesus answered and said unto them,
Elijah truly shall first come, and restore all things."
Matthew 17:11

"But their minds were blinded…" II Corinthians 3:14

Dear Child,

Partial belief is unbelief. For this reason, many do not see nor recognize My miracles and My supernatural interventions. However, I am gifting many with My gift of faith to trust Me radically and wholly. I am demonstrating My power and truth around your world in preparation for the great ingathering. No place is too remote for My gospel to reach. No one is too small or weak to be a part. Many will be willing to give all, including their lives, for this endeavor. Be at peace in your place of direct influence, and take courage to do what I guide you to do for others. Recognition is not needed and would often be an obstacle or hindrance to My purpose. Obscure and hidden soldiers are battle tactics that I originated and still use. Don't be weary in My discipline, training, and deployment. I am also the final, overseeing general, victorious leader!

Jesus said, *"…the harvest is the end of the world…." Matthew 13:39*

*"And they overcame him by the blood of the lamb,
and by the word of their testimony;
and they loved not their lives unto the death." Revelation 12:11*

Dear Child,

All is well, child, in My Kingdom. Hold firm in what you know to be true. Breathe deep of My calming peace. Rebuke the one who condemns and forgive those who misunderstand or use you in their pain and fear. I am the close Friend who affirms and holds you dear. Draw on Me. Wait on Me to defend and protect you. It's My approval and faithfulness that are real and sustaining. Let minor soulish concerns go, and enjoy your fellowship with Me and My rich blessings all around you. There's healing and peace under My wings.

"…there is a friend that sticks closer than a brother." Proverbs 18:24

"He shall cover you with His feathers, and under His wings shall you trust: His truth shall be your shield and buckler." Psalm 91:4

Dear Child,

I am your healer. Healing is My original design for mankind. My keeping power maintains all life in an unseen balance. You do well to call upon Me in all sickness, distress, and need. I hold back nothing good from those who walk closely with Me. I give you much compassion for those who suffer without Me. You do well to teach others to call upon Me and depend upon Me. Continue to keep your focus on Me and what I say. Do not be anxious for the condition of your world, created by sinful, blind, selfish people.

"For the Lord God is a sun and shield:
the Lord will give grace and glory:
no good thing will He with hold from them that walk uprightly."
Psalm 84:11

"Let the Word of Christ dwell in you richly in all wisdom;
teaching and admonishing one another..." Colossians 3:16

Dear Child,

You cannot force anyone to see and hear Me as you do. You relating to Me is your path. Pushing and compelling are not My methods. Each must come to Me willingly, humbly confessing their need as a hopeless sinner. Your heart wants the best for others, but I must be the agent of invitation and revelation. Keep yourself from the world's pressure to perform, produce and see quick results. As always, I am gentle in My timing and gracious methods.

"For all have sinned, and come short of the glory of God" Romans 3:23

"But You, O Lord, are a God full of compassion, and gracious and
longsuffering, and plenteous in mercy and truth." Psalm 86:15

Dear Child,

Do not fear nor resist the changes I bring to your life seasons. Remain vibrant, interested in all I am doing in you and others. I'm always creating, making you into a matriarch, a mother to My people, able to see ahead and help Me guide them into My path of life. Walk on with dignity and purpose, whatever the response of others might be. Do not fear to examine the depths of potential sin in your heart. Bring all to My light. No man can then bring you to shock or despair. I nurture those who are willing to go to higher and higher places in Me. I stand guard at your heart to give you My thoughts.

"...I arose a mother in Israel." Judges 5:7

*"Examine yourselves whether you be in the faith;
prove your own selves..." II Corinthians 13:5*

Dear Child'

Enjoy this silence with Me. Let My peace overtake your mind, lift your heart and heal your weary body. This is the Sabbath I ordained, knowing how much you would need it. All need just to be, and experience My closeness, and closeness to all that I have created. Through ages of tradition and religion, many have forgotten their place as My children. They have forgotten that I value their relationship with Me above all external routines and rituals. This simplicity allows for all to come to Me to partake of My saving grace.

*"And the work of righteousness shall be peace;
and the effect of righteousness quietness and assurance forever.'
Isaiah 32:17*

"There remains therefore a rest to the people of God." Hebrews 4:9

Dear Child,

When mankind finds itself in the endless troubles possible on earth, questions arise about My reality and care. Without knowledge of and relationship with Me, bearing pain and suffering is seldom redemptive. I offer a way out and strength to endure, but it must be sought and desired. Man's escaping measures and refusal to suffer lead to the great confusion, illness, and tragedy you see daily on earth. My sacrifice on the cross provides for every human need.

"Though He were a Son, yet learned He obedience by the things which He suffered." Hebrews 5:8

"For we ourselves were sometimes foolish, disobedient, deceived, serving diverse lusts and pleasures, living in malice and envy, hateful and hating one another. But after that the kindness and love of God our Savior toward man appeared." Titus 3:3-4

Dear Child,

I am teaching you much about your inner self at this time. Take the time, much time, to listen and consider new insights by My Spirit. There's no standing still in comfort and complacency as you hold fast to Me. I move you on to victory after victory over yourself, sin, and the past. Resist not, and release all fear of the outcome. I know what I envision, and you will ultimately greatly rejoice with Me and My results, temporal and eternal.

"...though our outward man perish, yet the inward man is renewed day by day. For our light affliction, which is but for a moment, works for us a far more exceeding and eternal weight of glory." II Corinthians 4:16-17

"But thanks be to God, which gives us the victory through our Lord Jesus Christ." I Corinthians 15:57

Dear Child,

Have I not ordained the life process of seed to bloom and produce more fruit with seed? In the final seed is all the accumulated living done previously. Some can receive and know what they contain. Often, it requires a lifetime for eyes to open to My reality, My Kingdom, My extraordinary gift in every and all life. Rejoice that you are a repository of this deep wisdom, truth, and joy. Share it with those thirsty, seeking for Me and real life.

*"Jesus said, …He that sows the good seed is the Son of man;
the field is the world; the good seed are the children of the Kingdom…"
Matthew 13:37-38*

"Ho, everyone that thirsts, come to the waters…" Isaiah 55:1

Dear Child,

I give you the oil of joy for mourning. Release all sadness, regrets, losses to Me. One by one, you will learn to rejoice in My work and purposes in these. Your comprehension of Me and My justice and mercy will cause only wonder and joy to your heart. As My sunlight moves through your life, these shadows will disappear and have no more power in you. Remember, you are ever learning about My love, even in what seems hard and unjust to you. I am perfect in all My ways.

*"To appoint unto them that mourn in Zion, to give unto them
beauty for ashes, the oil of joy for mourning,
the garment of praise for the spirit of heaviness;
that they might be called trees of righteousness, the planting of the Lord,
that He might be glorified." Isaiah 61:3*

*"For You will light my candle: the Lord my God will enlighten
my darkness. As for God, His way is perfect…" Psalm 18:28, 30*

Dear Child,

Notice how your soul leaps in response to the brilliant, warm sunny day. You bring some of this to others when they see your open smiling face, and feel your warm, loving heart. I am your relational Father God. I desire My children to avoid isolation but to be, first of all, close to Me and willing to pay the price of close relationships with others. This is where My spiritual work and transformation are tested. Will you allow Me to love your neighbor as yourself, with My help and fruit?

Jesus said, *"For where two or three are gathered together in My Name, there am I in the midst of them."* Matthew 18:20

Jesus said, *"...You shall love your neighbor as yourself."* Matthew 22:39

Dear Child and Friend,

You have My compassion for the ills of your world; all that appears wrong, disordered, and perverse due to man's blind, sinful selfishness. But, remember, this is temporary. There is perfect order, perfect justice, perfect beauty, and health in My Kingdom, all motivated by My perfect love. Keep your affection and attention focused on Me and these things above as you live your life on earth. This keeps you close to Me and far from disappointment and despair. Your faith in Me and My goodness holds you in hope and gives you an increased capacity for love and a joyful heart.

"Set your affection on things above, not on things on the earth. For you are dead, and your life is hid with Christ in God." Colossians 3:2-3

"A merry heart does good like a medicine: but a broken spirit dries the bones." Proverbs 17:22

Dear Child,

What a haven is My peace in your world of turbulent storms; they needn't cause you to shake nor lose balance. Above the earth's weather is My clear air and light. I give you My peace freely as you adhere to My righteous leading, looking for the deep joy to follow. The everyday routine of ordinary needs and demands is the best place to draw on My endless peace. Keep yourself from envy, covetousness, and greed. These are easy snares to take My peace. Be content in your Father's abundant Kingdom of the true riches and life eternal.

"For You have been a strength to the poor,
a strength to the needy in his distress,
a refuge from the storm, a shadow from the heat,
when the blast of the terrible ones is as a storm against the wall."
Isaiah 25:4

"But godliness with contentment is great gain.
For we brought nothing into this world, and
it is certain we can carry nothing out." I Timothy 6:6-7

Dear Child,

When I speak to you so freely, it's to encourage your spirit to be full of My life, your entire lifetime. Let no dullness nor emptiness be your portion. I am always nourishing you and building up your whole being to a ripeness. The intention of the farmer is always a harvest and much increase of new seed to sow. This is My intention as well. This is the seed of My truth and wisdom lived out for others to see and desire in your human example. So, enjoy the wonders of growing in the knowledge of Me and giving it liberally.

"As you have therefore received Christ Jesus the Lord,
so walk you in Him: Rooted and built up in Him,
and established in the faith, as you have been taught,
abounding therein with thanksgiving." Colossians 2:6-7

Jesus said, *"...freely you have received, freely give." Matthew 10:8*

Dear Child of Mine,

Each one of My created persons has the deep need to know My love. Often, this is unknown to them and covered by their early experiences of love towards them. Human love is in some way flawed or even a negative experience. This can help or hinder their search for knowing Me and My love. In My wise Fatherly love, I sent a striking, undeniable sign of My love for humanity. I sent My only Son to be a sacrifice; for their eyes to see how great My love is for them. My love is unchanging, always the same.

"For I am the Lord, I change not..." Malachi 3:6

Jesus said, *"And this is the will of Him that sent Me, that every one which sees the Son, and believes on Him, may have everlasting life: and I will raise him up at the last day." John 6:40*

Dear Child of Mine,

As you consider your world and My speaking through examples and symbols, learn of Me afresh. Consider gold and how many live and die to possess it. Gold reflects light and has much beauty and weight. It is costly to acquire and often needs purification. Likewise, the true gold I make available is acquired through pain and purification. My wisdom, shining through humility, patience, love, and gentleness, is the gold I value most. I wish that My people would desire the true riches and see all earth as a shadow of what is real in My eternal Kingdom.

"Happy is the man that finds wisdom, and the man that gets understanding. For the merchandise of it is better than the merchandise of silver, and the gain thereof than fine gold." Proverbs 3:13-14

"Who gave Himself for us, that He might redeem us from all iniquity, and purify unto Himself a peculiar people, zealous of good works." Titus 2:14

Dear, Dear Child,

What adventures we have together as I send you to serve My special assignments of love and joy. You bring hope in Me even in the most humble, mundane, quiet service. I work in gradual, small, often unnoticed ways in the lives of My children. While they are about obedience to My leading and thinking, I am transforming them to Myself. I am also using them as a powerful stimulation to growth and healing in others. In My economy, all are enriched and made whole in relationship to Me and others.

Jesus said, *"Truly, truly, I say unto you,*
He that receives whomsoever I send receives Me,
and he that receives Me receives Him that sent Me." John 13:20

"If you be willing and obedient, you shall eat the good of the land."
Isaiah 1:19

My Dear Child,

I am bringing you into greater wholeness. You are learning My ways as you reflect on your experiences, memories, and patterns of behavior. All this gives you a reserve of understanding of yourself and others. When I say wisdom is better to get than gold, I mean for you to value it and glean it. Therefore, you have established hope when you know that I have something good to give in every experience. Lay up these treasures for your heavenly life and be rich in wisdom for your earthly life.

"I will remember the works of the Lord:
surely I will remember Your wonders of old.
I will meditate also of all your work, and talk of your doings."
Psalm 77:11-12

Jesus said, *"But lay up for yourselves treasures in heaven,*
where neither moth nor rust does corrupt, and
where thieves do not break through nor steal:
For where your treasure is, there will your heart be also." Matthew 6:20-21

Dear Child of Mine,

Have I not created you with the capacity to laugh and be merry? This is for your well-being, release, and joy. Your ability to see contrasts, absurdities, and consequences is part of My nature in you. Your brain is more complex and wondrous than you can ever imagine. My great desire as a Father is for My children to enjoy Me and all the good and beautiful I have created. I love the sound of happy laughter and good gatherings of My children. There needs to be a balance of sobriety and laughter in My family.

"I will praise You; for I am fearfully and wonderfully made; marvelous are your works; and that my soul knows right well."
Psalm 139:14

"A merry heart does good like a medicine" *Psalm 17:22*

Dear Child,

Your heart longs for the end of winter as your thoughts imagine the bright daffodils waiting, hidden in your garden. Just so, is My fresh love for you each day of your life. Therefore, I say to you often, wait upon Me, My perfect timing and opportunities. From your side of time, the waiting may seem incomprehensible. It's a call to closer intimacy with Me. I have much that you can understand if you choose to listen and learn; receive the revelation of Me you need first. I am often waiting on you too.

"Rest in the Lord, and wait patiently for Him...." *Psalm 37:7*

"But it is good for me to draw near to God...." *Psalm 73:28*

Dear Child,

Have I not tilted the earth in such a way as to pour glorious sunshine to you? There can be no doubt of My sovereign order to all you see and experience. This evidence is too wide and deep for you to comprehend. It speaks of My love for you as an individual of great value, proceeding in the long family line of humanity I have created. As a child who enjoys parents, family, and home, I desire you to enjoy Me in wonder, also the earth home and family where I have placed you. See this new season as a surprise gift.

"So shall they fear the name of the Lord from the west, and His glory from the rising of the sun..." Isaiah 59:19

"I will sing of the mercies of the Lord forever: with my mouth will I make known Your faithfulness to all generations." Psalm 89:1

Dear Child,

Do not expect a life without trials and trouble. This is not possible, not to your advantage. Much seems unjust to you. Yes, there is great injustice and dark sin in the world. For you, I must allow the outcomes of sin to be evident, much as a living lesson and a way to teach My truth. Sadly, the rebellious, ignorant and selfish must often suffer as the prodigal son, bringing pain to all concerned. In this, the universal sin nature is made evident, and the door is then open for My vast forgiveness, redemption, and loving restoration. Find encouragement in this.

"God is our refuge and strength, a very present help in trouble." Psalm 46:1

"Behold, the days come, says the Lord, that I will raise unto David a righteous Branch, and a King shall reign and prosper, and shall execute judgment and justice in the earth." Jeremiah 23:5

Dear Child of Mine,

These are days of tremendous pressure on My faithful people. These are times to gather and hold together. All are growing in different life seasons amidst the darkness and hardness of the time. There must be encouragement from one to another as evil darkness tries to encroach. Facing truth with My mind is far better than escaping into the many ways possible and too readily available. My people are shining My light across the world to those yet to come to Me. Be part of My heart and hand extended. Pay willingly and gladly the price of being My disciple.

"And let us consider one another
to provoke unto love and to good works:
Not forsaking the assembling of ourselves together,
as the manner of some is; but exhorting one another:
and so much the more, as you see the day approaching."
Hebrews 10:24-25

Jesus said,
"...Go you into all the world, and preach the gospel to every creature."
Mark 16:15

Dear Child,

Yes, I have said, "Pray for them which despitefully use you, and persecute you." Persecution happens as I allow sinful human nature to expose itself. Among the many forms of suffering this causes is the loss of reputation at the hands and mouth of those who cannot see their need of being saved from themselves. But, rejoice at the long-suffering you are exercising as My child. Be assured that I, your defender and rewarder, am coming to your comfort and ultimate justice. Look to Me to bring good from these sufferings.

"Let this mind be in you,
which was also in Christ Jesus: Who, being in the form of God,
thought it not robbery to be equal with God:
But made Himself of no reputation,
and took upon Him the form of a servant,
and was made in the likeness of men." Philippians 2:5-7

Paul said, "I therefore, the prisoner of the Lord, beseech you
that you walk worthy of the vocation wherewith you are called.
With all lowliness and meekness,
with long-suffering, forbearing one another in love.
Endeavoring to keep the unity of the Spirit in the bond of peace."
Ephesians 4:1-3

Dear Child,

You will always go with fullness, never empty-handed. And when you come to Me, your baskets, your storehouse will overflow. Enjoy being My hands, creating good wherever you are. All My promises are yes, amen, and cannot be measured. I enjoy your fellowship, your dependence, and co-laboring with Me. Be encouraged that I use it all, much more than you see or can imagine. My name means Mighty God, All Provider. Yes, you are in an excellent place to grow and attend to My garden, My people. Give without hesitancy.

"Blessed shall be your basket and your store." Deuteronomy 28:5

Jesus said, *"…It is more blessed to give than to receive."* Acts 20:35

Dear Child,

Yes, live in expectancy of Me always. Expect Me to answer your prayers in ways and times only I can determine. Be of good cheer. I keep Israel, and I do not slumber nor sleep. Rest. Recognize the ebb and flow of activity and rest. Remember, I am Sovereign. I raise up, and I bring down, I add, I remove. I still have much for you to do and give. Quietly serve, quietly pray, observe and fill up what is lacking. I am tender with you, dear aging one, and I want you to be tender with yourself and others. All is well. All moves in My oscillating order. I know your heart that beats with Mine.

"Let the heavens be glad, and let the earth rejoice: and let men say among the nations, the Lord reigns." I Chronicles 16:31

"And be kind to one another, tenderhearted, forgiving one another, even as God for Christ's sake has forgiven you." Ephesians 4:32

Dear Child,

I am way ahead of you, helping you weigh everything, weighing your words, responses, and motives. Yes, I am the One bringing reproof and discipline into your life at this season. Always be ready to learn and grow up more in Me. Yield, and take more time in My Presence to meditate and rest. I have much more for you.

We *"...speaking the truth in love, may grow up into Him in all things, which is the head, even Christ."* Ephesians 4:15

"All scripture is given by inspiration of God, and is profitable for doctrine, for reproof, for correction, for instruction in righteousness: that the man of God may be perfect, thoroughly furnished unto all good works." II Timothy 3:16-17

Dear Child,

I am not hard pressing on you. Do not be so hard on yourself. I've forgiven your sins as you asked and given you My gift of repentance. Now, go on and avoid these small transgressions. I allow you the little blessings that a Father provides. I want you to truly feel My protection and direction you lacked personally as a child. I am working deep balance in your soul. Receive it. My thoughts are to be your motive and message. Keep your heart clean of wrong thoughts by resting in Me. No pressure, no striving to be good or do good. I am your goodness, and you simply follow Me, My thoughts, My actions. As always, we must work together.

"The Lord is not slack concerning His promise, as some men count slackness; but is long-suffering towards us, not willing that any should perish, but that all should come to repentance." II Peter 3:9

"Create in me a clean heart, O God; and renew a right Spirit within me." Psalm 51:10

Dear Child,

Be comforted. No striving, no comparison, no competition is needed. As a true Father loves each child, so I love you. Nothing can separate us. You needn't be conformed to this world. Rejoice in who I created you to be. Give others the courage to be real, alive in Me, and free to rejoice also. Be not ashamed. Be free in Me. I took all your shame.

"For we dare not make ourselves of the number, or compare ourselves with some that commend themselves; but they measuring themselves by themselves, and comparing themselves among themselves, are not wise." II Corinthians 10:12

"In You, O Lord, do I put my trust; let me never be ashamed: deliver me in your righteousness." Psalm 31:1

Dear Child,

Yes, the world, to your earthly observations, often appears bleak, cold, forbidding. I must allow My children to choose. I would have it be different, as I originally intended. This is where you need to take courage and the gift of faith in Me. Turn your eyes to My glorious Kingdom and Me in the warmth, beauty, and heart comfort I provide. Hear Me in the quiet; see Me in My created people and surroundings. It is all more than you can understand, but I continue, unmoved in My order, change and love. You can depend upon this and be secure. I do have strong, eternal arms.

"Of the increase of His government and peace there shall be no end, upon the throne of David, and upon His Kingdom, to order it, and to establish it with judgment and with justice from henceforth even for ever. The zeal of the Lord of hosts will perform this." Isaiah 9:7

"The eternal God is your refuge, and underneath are the everlasting arms...." Deuteronomy 33:27

Be of good cheer, My child,

It is not your work to fix or find solutions to the problems of others. Apparent needs are not always the actual needs. Only I see the entire picture. Be at peace as we grow together day by day, and I use you in what will be some extended processes of transformations. Wrap My Spirit around you like a mantle in comfort, patience, joy, and peace.

Jesus said, *"...Be of good cheer; it is I; be not afraid." Matthew 14:27*

"The Spirit of the Lord God is upon me...;
To appoint unto them that mourn in Zion,
to give them beauty for ashes, the oil of joy for mourning,
the garment of praise for the spirit of heaviness;
that they might be called trees of righteousness,
the planting of the Lord,
that He might be glorified." Isaiah 61:1-3

Dear Child,

Few take notice of My hand turning the earth about the sun, giving night and day, rest and activity to My creation. Let gratitude pour up to Me from your tender heart for all My majestic, incomparable handiwork and care for the earth. Oh, if men would see their place in My plan as children, and be thankful to know Me, what peace and beauty would touch all mankind. Take courage and rest in Me, My dear child, I hear your heart's cry for so many, and I care. Wait and watch in trust of Me.

"From the rising of the sun unto the going down of the same
the Lord's name is to be praised." Psalm 113:3

"The Spirit itself bears witness with our spirit,
that we are the children of God." Romans 8:16

Dear Child,

Reflection will reveal that all your imperfections are not corrected at once. I work with the most needful ones first. I comfort you as a Father comforts a growing, learning child. Repent, repent, repent until Christ forms a new righteous pattern in you. Be My happy child, secure in My love. And remember, I am correcting all My children.

"For Godly sorrow works repentance to salvation not to be repented of: but the sorrow of the world works death." II Corinthians 7:10

"My son, despise not the chastening of the Lord; neither be weary of His correction." Proverbs 3:11

Dear Child,

What man calls dancing is an unrestrained delight in being My creation, even among those who do not know Me. Childlike freedom only can be expressed by moving to a rhythm of joy. Music is a gift from heaven, an attempt at recreating My sounds as all moves in My universe. Some even express My radiant, warm sun in their smiles, as My sun's warmth is My smile of pleasure and love. Enjoy My goodness. Your responses delight Me.

"Let them praise His Name in the dance: let them sing praises unto Him with the timbrel and harp." Psalm 149:3

"The Lord make His face shine upon you, and be gracious unto you." Numbers 6:25

Dear Child,

Radiate My love in your sense of well-being, security, and peace. Think on Me, your complete source. This keeps your focus on the present now. You do not need to compare, compete, or criticize. As you can see, all is well in My Kingdom. You can rejoice as My child, under My care, depending, leaning, and waiting on Me.

*"... The love of God is shed abroad in our hearts
by the Holy Spirit which is given unto us."
Romans 5:5*

*"Being confident of this very thing,
that He which began a good work in you
will perform it until the day of Jesus Christ." Philippians 1:6*

Dear Child,

There are ordained seasons of growth and change for all. There are human limitations in all of life's seasons. Keep My perspective as you support and honor those in seasons before and after you. Each person is a link with something to give. Recognize what you need and what you lack to serve My people, young and old. Ask, and it shall be given to you. Be a good listener, receiver, and giver.

*"Be kindly affectionate to one another with brotherly love;
in honor preferring one another." Romans 12:10*

*"Ask, and it shall be given to you; seek and you shall find;
knock and it shall be opened unto you." Matthew 7:7*

Dear Child,

Yes, you have released an old, childish idea of My making everything right in this world now. This is how a child looks to a father. Now, as you look to Me as your heavenly Father, you see the true source of that idea; My perfection, justice, and righteousness. Continue to enjoy learning of Me now, before you meet me in eternity. Always die to your own opinions and understanding.

"He is the Rock,
His work is perfect:
for all His ways are judgment:
a God of truth and without iniquity, just and right is He."
Deuteronomy 32:4

"Trust in the Lord with all your heart; and lean not unto your own understanding. In all your ways acknowledge Him, and He shall direct your paths." Proverbs 3:5-6

Dear Child,

Be teachable, be alert to those around you. See them with My mind and heart. Draw on My timing and ways to bring My life to them. Perhaps a prayer, words or actions that speak of Me and how well I know them and care about them. I make you a ready friend and servant. I write your story and that of others in this way.

"Preach the word; be instant in season, out of season... "
II Timothy 4:2

Jesus said, *"...If any man desire to be first,*
the same shall be last of all, and servant of all." Mark 9:35

Dear Child,

Yes, much healing happens that is neither understood nor appreciated. Be one who recognizes My healing power in the many ways I accomplish it. In most cases, healing of spirit and soul is what is needed. I am the Great Physician, Savior, and Reconciler, and I hear the cries and prayers of the sick and lost. My compassion and mercy go to the broken, the contrite, and the suffering ones of My children. I reconcile hearts, people, nations, and physical bodies and draw together what needs to be joined.

"The sacrifices of God are a broken spirit:
a broken and contrite heart, O God, You will not despise." Psalm 51:17

"For it pleased the Father that in Him should all fullness dwell;
And having made peace through the blood of His cross,
by Him to reconcile all things unto Himself; by Him, I say,
whether they be things in earth, or things in heaven."
Colossians 1:19-20

Dear Child,

Yes, all your springs are in Me; all you have and will receive on earth comes from My hand of love. Don't trouble yourself trying to understand all you experience. Let Me lead, reveal, and use you as I wisely know best. There is much you cannot comprehend outside of heaven. Keep in My peace, enjoy My wonders, remembering you are My dear child, and all is well with your Father. I am the Repairer, Restorer, and Healer as I know best.

"...all my springs are in You." Psalm 87:7

"...I am the Lord that heals you." Exodus 15:26

Dear Child,

Your writing pleases Me. I will use the words I give you to speak to many, training them to hear My voice also. This will bring riches untold to individuals, families, people groups. Leave all to Me, and continue to place on paper all I say to you. These are times when many hunger for wellsprings of hope and faith. I provide abundantly through the willing, My child.

"…my tongue is the pen of a ready writer." Psalm 45:1

"I will make Your Name to be remembered in all generations: therefore shall the people praise You forever and ever." Psalm 45:17

Dear Child,

Today, as every day, I am close and comforting, as you receive. Be not troubled by the sufferings of this world. I am at work to reveal Myself to those who call upon Me. Many bring consequences of suffering upon themselves and others because they refuse Me. Oft times, man can only discover Me through suffering. Be at peace, appreciating Me as the Good Shepherd, looking after earth and My sheep who cannot thrive without My care and oversight. Be content to follow Me and seek My best for all. Love, love, love, and feed My sheep.

Jesus said, *"I am the good shepherd: the good shepherd gives His life for the sheep." John 10:11*

Jesus said, *"My sheep hear My voice, and I know them, and they follow Me." John 10:27*

Yes, Child,

Your tree is planted by My river of the water which is My Spirit. Yes, you have, and will continue to have, fresh "sap" rising that I can and will use. Do not relegate yourself to inactive, old age. I have much for you to do and be for others. Trust My sufficiency.

"And he shall be like a tree planted by the rivers of water,
that brings forth his fruit in his season;
his leaf also shall not wither; and whatsoever he does shall prosper."
Psalm 1:3

"Those that be planted in the house of the Lord
shall flourish in the courts of our God.
They shall bring forth fruit in old age;
they shall be fat and flourishing."
Psalm 92:13-14

Dear Child,

My heart bursts with love for this world. Your heart feels My love for this world. It is necessary that we agree and that you respond as I would to the pain, disorder, and darkness. Please remember, you are My child, and I would have you in good balance, in the world, but not of it. Don't focus on the black and white of the fallen world. Enjoy the beauty, perfection, and justice of My gloriously colored Kingdom. Enjoy, My child. Enjoy Me.

"For God so loved the world, that He gave His only begotten Son,
that whosoever believes in Him should not perish,
but have everlasting life." John 3:16

"They are not of the world, even as I am not of the world." John 17:16

Two Days before Christmas

Dear Child,

Rejoice in a new day of possibilities with Me. Even in the coldest of winters, I would have you to reach and give out. Your natural tendency might be to withdraw and be introspective, but I would have you reach for the warmth of human and Divine fellowship. This is the season of giving, and I enjoy your imitation of Me in giving generously of my endless supply of heart motivation, choosing to delight others, and surprise them that someone knows and cares about their well-being and value. My thoughts are like this and endless.

"Hereby perceive we the love of God, because He laid down His life for us: and we ought to lay down our lives for the brethren.' I John 3:16

"Many, O Lord my God are your wonderful works which You have done, and Your thoughts which are towards us :
they cannot be reckoned up in order unto You:
if I would declare and speak of them,
they are more than can be numbered." Psalm 40:5

Dear Child,

What greater gift could be given than My Son: My gift that continually gives every other good gift? Rejoice that you partner with Me in this labor to give Myself to others. I fill your heart to overflowing, seeing the unfolding transformation of lives surrendered to My will. I have greater gifts for you, My child, that you cannot even dream of at this time. I know every desire you have, and have put aside to be a giver to others. I have created you to find your place as one who nurtures My good growth in others. I do not forget you, and your reward is, and shall be great!

"Blessed be the Lord, who daily loads us with benefits,
even the God of our salvation..." Psalm 68:19

"...Truly there is a reward for the righteous:
truly He is a God that judges in the earth.' Psalm 58:11

Dear Child,

Your life cannot always be in full bloom. There are the waning years that all must experience. These are years of less intense activity, lending themselves to greater meditation and reflection. You can learn much in this way. Quiet withdrawal is often the most fruitful choice. As you agree with Me in your thoughts and prayers, you can accomplish much. Abiding with Me makes a rich, fruitful life in all its seasons. All are essential. There is an element of sadness, as you would like to see Me prevailing in lives and situations being destroyed and harmed. There you join Me in My sufferings. We comfort one another in hope and trust for My coming to make all things new.

Jesus said, *"Abide in Me, and I in you.*
As the branch cannot bear fruit of itself, except it abide in the vine;
no more can you, except you abide in Me." John 15:4

And He that sat upon the throne said, Behold I make all things new."
Revelation 21:5

Yes, Dear Child,

You have made the transition to less of you, more of Me. Self still resists at times, yet you experience My deep joy and power as you relinquish your all to Me. You then experience how useless your desires for this or that which will not truly satisfy. The peace I am giving you is beyond anything the world can give you now. Simply follow My Spirit day by day, quietly, step by delightful step, without concern for what others do or think. Here is the comfort you ask of Me! Your times are in My hands. Have no fear. Be steadfast. Believe Me, not what you see. Relish and use the obscure, hidden life with Me as this is where I've led you. Don't look back. This is My goal for you.

"He must increase, but I must decrease." John 3:30
"My times are in Your hand..." Psalm 31:15

Dear Child,

Believe Me when I say your scarlet sins have been made white as snow. Be delivered from all guilt and shame. I see you as cleansed. Take heart; I am reigning in your life; I go before you to order your steps. There is much to oppose you and distract you, but I am holding your hand. Cling to Me and know My comfort. Let all these lesser concerns go as you concentrate on Me and My ways. I am for you, and the thoughts of others are of no importance. My inner light and the oil of joy sustaining you needs to be shining and evident. The rest is My work and purpose fulfilled.

"Come now, and let us reason together, says the Lord: though your sins be as scarlet, they shall be as white as snow; though they be red like crimson, they shall be as wool." Isaiah 1:18

"...If God be for us, who can be against us?" Romans 8:31

Dear Child,
I hear, I help, and I hold you close. I give My peace and good will
to you. No weapon formed against you shall prosper. Continue in
child-like faith to live in Me, dependent, hopeful, waiting. I deliver
by safely guiding you through narrow channels. It may appear a
restrictive life, but it is My safe way for you—no envy of the way
of wealth and glamour. I release you from all guilt, shame, and
dishonor of failure and weakness. Rejoice in this cleansing, freedom,
and renewal. I speak to you of rest, of quiet and peace. Receive all,
and enjoy it. I place no pressure on you, no position, or image to
uphold. My desire for you and your household is a hidden life with
Me—far from the dark chaos and close to Me.

Jesus said, *"Because straight is the gate, and narrow is the way,*
which leads unto life, and few there be that find it."
Matthew 7:14

"But if we walk in the light, as He is in the light,
we have fellowship one with another,
and the blood of Jesus Christ His Son cleanses us from all sin."
I John 1:7

Dear Child,

Yes, I say stand when all is in My order; then hold fast to Me. Stay steady, stay balanced and available to Me, whatever you may hear or see of plagues, storms, and dissolution of that which seemed so fixed. In Me and My Word and Kingdom, set your security. Be an example to those whose hearts may fail them in fear. Extend My hope, comfort, and truth. My words never fail. Be one who does not give up on all the challenges. Much will occur as a result of man's foolish denial of Me and My unchanging truth. Out of the resulting suffering and loss, I bring new, real-life salvation and restoration.

"Wherefore take unto you the whole armor of God,
that you may be able to withstand in the evil day,
and having done all, to stand."
Ephesians 6:13

Jesus said, *"Men's hearts failing them for fear,*
and for looking after those things which are coming on the earth:
for the powers of heaven shall be shaken."
Luke 21:26

Dear Child,

My words bring life. There is no end to My speaking, and never will be. I was, and am and will ever be. In My great love for you, I am always available to speak. Would that all men would listen and hear Me. Take comfort and have no fear for the days ahead. All time is in My hands. Events on earth will and must eventually grow more dark and ominous. This is inevitable, as I expose men's hearts, and the need for One to save them; save them from their weak and hopeless selves. In all this, My strength and hope will shine like a lighthouse, showing where to turn safely. Rejoice in all I will do to show the world that I am who I say I am.

"Jesus Christ the same yesterday, and today, and forever."
Hebrews 13:8

"And God said unto Moses, I AM that I AM...."
Exodus 3:14

Jesus said, *"Fear not, little flock;*
for it is your Father's good pleasure to give you the Kingdom."
Luke 12:32